THE RAVENGLASS & ESKDALE RAILWAY

W. J. K. DAVIES

DAVID & CHARLES
NEWTON ABBOT LONDON NORTH POMFRET (VT)

Library of Congress Catalog Card Number 81-65680

British Library Cataloguing in Publication Data

Davies, W. J. K. (William James Keith), *1935–*
The Ravenglass & Eskdale railway. 3rd ed.
1. Cumbria. Eskdale. Narrow gauge railway
services: Ravenglass & Eskdale Railway,
to 1980
I. Title
385′.52′0942784

ISBN 0-7153-9224-7

First published 1968
Second edition 1981

Printed in Great Britain
by Redwood Burn Ltd Trowbridge Wiltshire
for David & Charles (Publishers) Limited
Brunel House Newton Abbot Devon

Published in the United States of America
by David & Charles Inc
North Pomfret Vermont 05053 USA

Contents

Illustrations

IN TEXT

Author's Notes and Acknowledgments

It is not often these days that an author has the pleasure of chronicling a British minor railway that is still flourishing, especially one that still provides a year-round service. Add to this the most peculiar history of the Ravenglass & Eskdale Railway and the task is quite fascinating. For the line was in Chancery less than a year after it opened to passengers, saw its main source of traffic die out within ten years and yet survived another twenty-seven, suffering metamorphosis into the short-lived Eskdale Railway Company in the process. Its rotting remains were then first leased and then sold quite without authority to a third and most eccentric concern which itself was later 'taken over' in the best industrial fashion. It possessed a granite quarry which the 'new' management first promoted vigorously and then allowed to decline along with the railway slowly but surely for the next twenty-three years before selling out to yet another company. This was a granite-quarrying company which soon stopped quarrying on the R & E but ran it exclusively for passengers for several years before it in turn sold out to a preservation movement. Now the sixth management, backed by an enthusiastic owner and an ever-helpful preservation society, is raising the railway to heights undreamt-of before. For the first time in its life, it is even making substantial operating profits and, even more unusually, has recently received a brand-new locomotive.

Such a history cannot be other than fascinating to write, even if often frustrating through lack of records, and I am glad to have been asked to do so. This has really been a co-operative venture with the R & E R Company and the society for, without them and their whole-hearted co-operation, it could not have been written.

I would therefore like to pay tribute to all who have helped, and particularly to the following: Douglas Ferreira, the general manager, and Tom Jones, the Engineer, for undertaking much of the local research and for patiently reading, correcting, and often rewriting the script; the R & E staff (especially Dick Nicholson, up and down the valley on *Irt*); Geoff Toms, who produced the extremely atmospheric artistic sketches scattered throughout the book; Harry Buck for his excellent drawings of *Devon* and the *Ella* conversion; D. Ferreira again, for the 'Atlas' and P. G. Satow for gradient profile; G. Moser, F. H. Eyles, and A. Maclean of the preservation society who provided legal, financial, and local press information respectively and who made available all the research they had already done; Mr P. Le Neve Foster, MA, ARPS, for invaluable reminiscences of the Mitchell era; Mrs Hilton; Messrs C. J. Allen, J. L. Bate, H. Clayton, A. G. Langley, M. Murray, R. Nightingale, D. Pickup, E. Steel, W. Vaughan; The British Museum and the Public Records Office; The Leconfield Estate Co; the Joint Archives Committee for Cumberland, Westmorland and Carlisle, and the City Library, Carlisle; Mr D. Hay, Whitehaven Librarian. Lastly one must pay tribute to the late Mary C. Fair whose published writings and vast collection of photographs are essential for any chronicler of the R & E. I would particularly like to acknowledge the kindness of her executor, Miss Aileen Armstrong, in allowing us free use of this material.

For the revised edition I would like to record my thanks to all the R & ER staff and particularly to Peter van Zeller: Photographs are kindly acknowledged to the following by page numbers (a = upper photo; b = lower one): N. Bollans 45a; F. H. Eyles 134b; D. M. E. Ferreira 151, 152a; P. le Neve Foster 116b; H. G. W. Household 133b; Lancashire Evening Post 152b; J. M. Lloyd 35b; Sankey Ltd, Barrow 48b, 57a; the late W. H. Whitworth 75a; J. W. Wills (courtesy J. Harrison) 57b; R & ER collection 17a, 18a, 47; and G. T. Heavyside for the cover photograph. All the rest were taken by that indefatigable recorder of the lakeland scene, the late Mary C. Fair. Several of these were kindly lent by their present owner Mr Bert Thompson who also loaned many other views that shed light on the railway's history.

Second Edition

Indeed I would wish to thank all the railway staff for their friendship and general helpfulness, the editor of, and contributors to, the R & E R Newsletter for all their recording of events, and Douglas Ferreira, Graham Withers and Peter van Zeller for particular help. I am especially grateful to Peter who combines his railway work with 'curating' the museum and is constantly digging into the obscurer byways of Ratty's history—fortunately, so far, without invalidating anything major!

Additional photos courtesy R & E R.

CHAPTER 1

Inception of the Railway

BACKGROUND

The Ravenglass & Eskdale Railway, situated in one of the more remote parts of West Cumberland, has had probably the most involved history of any British minor line, and all its troubles have stemmed from its original purpose. That, for example, a railway built at considerable expense to transport a basic material, iron ore, to a neighbouring iron and steel industry should be in Chancery within a year of its opening and lose its main traffic only seven years later is almost incredible unless one knows something about the distribution of iron ore in these islands.

There are, in Britain, two types of iron ore-bearing stone. That most commonly worked is contained in the rich strata of ore found in the limestone wolds of North Oxfordshire, Leicestershire, and Northants. Here the ore lies in thick, easily-worked layers, often near the surface; but there is another form of iron ore, haematite, which is found in folds and pockets of the older granite rocks to the west of the country.

The disadvantage of this ore is that the deposits, formed under pressure when the rocks were young, exist only in erratic veins which often fade out almost without warning, or in isolated pockets in the rock. It is thus hard to win, often involving complicated mining, and the ore content is not particularly high. Yet in times of great demand any iron ore may be valuable and, in western Cumberland, within easy distance of the iron and steel towns such as Millom and Workington, there are fairly large haematite deposits; indeed these towns grew up because of their presence.

The easiest-won deposits are near the coast, but substantial quantities exist up side valleys. One such valley, or complex of valleys, is the group leading east from the ancient Roman port of

Ravenglass, in particular Eskdale and Miterdale; numerous lodes existing particularly in the fell between these two. The Romans knew of these deposits and worked them, and afterwards medieval smelters picked at the odd outcroppings where the ore came to the surface. But most of the ore is underground and difficulties of transport deterred any real explorations until the rise of the iron and steel industry in the eighteenth century created a considerable demand for iron ore.

Modern workings of iron ore in Eskdale appear to have been initiated during the first half of the nineteenth century, when a man named Lindow began work on the northern flank just opposite the King of Prussia Inn (now the Tatiegarth) in the location later known as Ban Garth, and at another location near the village of Boot some seven miles inland from Ravenglass. These were leased from the Leconfield estate.

The Boot project was abandoned after expensive mining operations had shown little result but for some years in the early 1850s Lindow made considerable attempts to extend the Ban Garth workings where a vein of ore had been proved, extending in a north-south direction through the fell. An average of around 1,500 tons of ore per annum was taken from this mine but, in 1854, the main lode petered out in solid granite and work ceased altogether. Nothing more was done until 1860, when another small operator, one Jos Fearon, re-opened Lindow's old mine and drove further levels into the hill below the former workings. He ran into the same troubles as his predecessor, the ore veins proving very impure and erratic and the cost of cartage to Drigg Station over rough roads being, at 4s 6d a ton, prohibitive. He appears to have suspended operations around 1863 and the workings were then deserted.

WHITEHAVEN IRON MINES LIMITED

About 1870, the demand for iron ore of any kind increased rapidly as a result of the Franco-Prussian war, and it seemed that the haematite deposits in Eskdale and similar valleys might well be profitably worked. The immediate result was the formation, on 19 January 1871, of Whitehaven Iron Mines Limited with a nominal capital of £95,000 in £10 shares.

> To purchase the interests of the present proprietor in two certain extensive Mineral Properties in the County of Cumberland and known respectively as the 'Eskdale and Miterdale Iron Mines' in the manors of Eskdale and Miterdale, and the 'Floutern Tarn,

Starling Dodd, and Red Pike Iron and Lead Mines', situate, lying and being within the manor of Loweswater.

Unlike its predecessors, the company was not a purely local concern for its sponsors included the Earl of Devon and one William White, a 'professor of chemistry in London' who presumably provided scientific glamour and possible expertise on the board. Its powers were sweeping, including the permission to 'construct railways and tramways; purchase rent or hire waggons; purchase rent or charter steam or sailing ships;' and to make any other arrangements necessary to allow it to mine and deal in ironstone or ore.

The company immediately negotiated to buy the right to work certain properties from its then lessor for the sum of £65,000, of which £50,000 was to be in the form of shares. The lessor, who went by the resounding Victorian name of Faithfull Cookson (of 9d New Bond Street, London, Ironmaster) was obviously an extremely canny character for he did very well out of the deal. Having sold what must have been simply the lease and any equipment for an excellent sum he then proceeded rapidly to dispose of all but £8,000 worth of his shares to other members of the company and, finally, only two years later in June 1873, he pulled out entirely, buying the Loweswater properties back for £30,000.

Thus not only did he make a clear £35,000 on the original deal, but he retained what from all accounts were the best properties – and to add to all this he made Whitehaven Iron Mines Limited take his remaining shares as part of the £30,000 purchase price for the Loweswater properties. Reading between the lines, it seems that the Mines company was not very happy about the whole position for the purchase agreement stipulated that if it had any trouble getting a new lease of the Eskdale rights from Lord Leconfield, Cookson would enforce his own agreement to do so.

In the event, a lease was granted for 25 years from 1873, the Mines company having already begun work under the old one in three places within our area—Ban Garth, Blea Tarn above Beckfoot, and the Nab Gill site at Boot, formerly explored by Lindow. Ban Garth, although the easiest site to work because the mines were already extensive and connected by a primitive incline to the valley below, proved unprofitable; the vein was almost exhausted and, when new levels driven in 1873-4 met with little success, the site appears to have been abandoned to allow concentration on the other two.

Blea Tarn lode, well up the hillside to the east of Ban Garth, provided some initial success, but the ore was merely a pocket in the hillside and the vein soon thinned to only seven or eight in. Tonnage gained was negligible, only 300 tons being won even in 1874 when the site was newly-opened. By 1881, it was virtually abandoned. There does not appear even to have been an incline, the ore presumably being brought out by pack-mule.

Nab Gill was different. Ore was soon proved in marketable quantities, sufficient to provide an average annual output of about 8,000 tons which, at the reigning price of 32s 6d a ton, was well worth having. In the next few years, no less than five levels were driven into the lode with varying success. Unfortunately, these mines were the farthest away from civilisation, requiring a haul of some nine miles by horse and cart to Drigg Station, which greatly reduced their profitability. In addition, the best ore was found near the fell top and it was necessary to construct an inclined plane, on the gauge of 2 ft, before even the rudimentary cart track at Boot could be reached.

PROMOTION OF THE RAILWAY

Something obviously had to be done to lessen these costs and, at a shareholders' meeting on 30 September 1872, it was decided to promote a Parliamentary Bill for 'a narrow gauge railway or tramway from the Eskdale Mines to Ravenglass (to be called the Ravenglass & Eskdale Railway)'. The Bill was duly promoted, although not as speedily as the impatient shareholders wished; they even called a special general meeting in London the following April to hasten things on but without in any way deflecting Parliament from its ponderous course.

Nevertheless, in the fullness of time the Ravenglass & Eskdale Railway (1873) Bill was duly approved and received the Queen's assent. It provided for the construction of a railway from Boot to a junction with the Furness Railway at Ravenglass Station, with a branch from Ravenglass down to the foreshore in the optimistic hope that traffic by sea might be possible. This branch was never built; the 'harbour' at Ravenglass, although well-known in Roman times, had long since silted up and, although occasional coasting schooners still called at the estuary, regular loading of iron ore would have required extensive dredging and building operations.

Both these railways were authorised to be built to a gauge of between 2 ft 9 in and standard, a provision which has since caused much heart-burning among historians. For legal reasons, a separate company, the Ravenglass & Eskdale Railway Company, was

Page 17: RAVENGLASS

[above] Early days: an unusual view of 'Nab Gill' and 3rd class coach awaiting departure from Ravenglass. [below] Much later view of 'Devon', recognisable by air pump on right running-plate, entering Ravenglass with passenger train. At the time, the tipping gantry was derelict, and the original of this photograph shows a fence across the end of the bank leading to the gantry

Page 18: UP THE LINE – I

[*above*] *'Nab Gill' at Boot Terminus. Note wagon in loading siding on left.* [*below*] *Up train at Beckfoot passenger platform. Note ore wagon and separate goods platform on down side with small shed*

incorporated by the Act to build and work them. The major shareholder in this was naturally Whitehaven Iron Mines Limited and the Mines company's secretary, J. W. Marshall, also acted as secretary to the railway; but the directors were not the same and the companies were separate entities. This was to be very important for the railway a few years later because it escaped closure when the mines went into liquidation.

Once the Act had been passed, the R & ER lost no time in

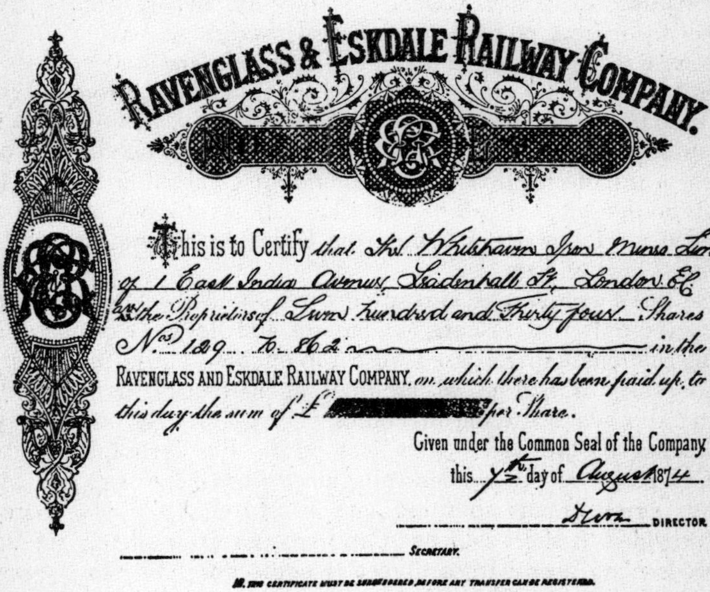

RAVENGLASS & ESKDALE RAILWAY COMPANY.

This is to Certify that The Whitehaven Iron Mines Limited of 1 East India Avenue, Leadenhall St, London EC is the Proprietor of Seven hundred and Thirty four Shares Nos. 129 to 862 in the RAVENGLASS AND ESKDALE RAILWAY COMPANY, on which there has been paid up to this day the sum of £ [redacted] per Share.

Given under the Common Seal of the Company this 7th day of August 1874.

DIRECTOR

SECRETARY.

N.B. This certificate must be surrendered before any transfer can be registered.

(1) *Share certificate of the original* R & E *Company*

initiating work on its main line. Of the issued capital of £24,000, half was taken up by the Iron Mines company and half by the contractor, Mr A. Oliver, who had recently finished building the Hemel Hempstead & Boxmoor Railway. In addition, the borrowing powers of £8,000 were all taken up over the next two years.

The railway was quite obviously conceived purely as a freight-carrying line, for its equipment and station facilities were clearly designed with this in mind. Eventually built to the 3 ft gauge (see Appendix 2) it began at a simple exchange wharf with the Furness Railway on the east side of Ravenglass Goods Yard.

The layout consisted simply of two dead-end sidings, one of

which paralleled an FR goods siding; the latter ran on to pass under a raised siding of the R & E from which ore could be discharged into standard-gauge wagons and which descended northward to join the R & E main line some distance from the station. The engine shed, a stone-built structure with two roads and a small workshop, was on the east side of the main line between the station and the point where the ore siding joined the main line. There was no run-round loop, and shunting must have been carried out by gravity or rope haulage—this was possible as the lines in the wharf yard sloped down from points near the road overbridge.

From Ravenglass the route then lay along the valley of the River Mite, running close alongside Muncaster Fell before entering Eskdale at the scattered hamlet of Eskdale Green, the only community of any size to be met *en route*. The present line, of which a full description will be found in Chapter 8, follows it closely so that all that will be noted here is that a public siding was provided at Hollowstones (now Irton Road) at the western end of Eskdale Green village.

The line's smithy was also situated here and the line itself ran on up the dale past Fisherground Farm and Beckfoot on varying grades before entering a last hard climb of about half-a-mile, some of it as steep as 1 in 34, to terminate at the foot of the Nab Gill incline above a scattering of houses referred to in contemporary documents as 'the Boot' (now just Boot). The layout here was more elaborate as the gradient of 1 in 70 was in the wrong direction to permit gravity shunting, and a run-round loop was therefore provided. A short siding ran on from this on the north side to an ore-loading dock with a tippler or chute from the mines tramway which was at a higher level.

THE OPENING TO TRAFFIC

The rails were laid through to Boot by April 1875 and, in this form, the railway was opened for goods traffic at the end of May with one locomotive and a number of wagons, the first customer apart from the iron mines being Mr J. Grave of the Bobbin Mill, near Eskdale Green, who used Irton Road siding. The exact date of opening is in doubt, Board of Trade records giving it as 24 May, while a letter from James Quan, the first General Manager, who was appointed at the beginning of May, gives it as 1 June. Quan was writing some forty years after the event so the earlier date is probably the more reliable.

In any case, the railway immediately proved its worth, no less than 6,378 tons of ore or ironstone being worked down to Ravenglass during the remainder of the year, and there was soon pressure from local inhabitants for the introduction of a passenger service. Accordingly, the company optimistically ordered two coaches and a van from the Bristol Wagon Company on extended credit and applied to the Board of Trade for permission to carry passengers.

The Board accordingly sent down its inspector of railways, Colonel Yolland, to make a formal inspection of the line on 29 June 1876. Alas! his report was even more scathing than usual for a minor railway. It is reproduced in full in Appendix 1 but, to put it briefly, the line was not in any shape for passenger services. Clearances were inadequate; only three—incomplete—stations were provided; there was only one locomotive; and, said the Colonel crushingly, he could not recollect having seen anywhere where the masonry was of such indifferent quality.

The directors were obviously taken aback and had a considerable quarrel with the contractor, who stated flatly that, as far as he was concerned, the line was finished and he did not intend to do any more. Judging from subsequent events, he was not keen to spend any more money on what for him was turning out to be an expensive business. Nevertheless, something had to be done.

The directors therefore authorised Quan to do what was necessary by direct labour. That energetic man promptly proceeded to complete the existing stations at Boot, Irton Road, and Ravenglass, and to install simpler waiting huts and short raised platforms at Beckton (sic), King of Prussia (now Eskdale Green), and Muncaster, meanwhile acquiring a second locomotive and running at least one unauthorised special train up the valley when, on 22 August, the Whitehaven Scientific Association came to view the mines and bobbin mills on one of those Victorian orgies of self-improvement.

The association was very impressed both with the line in general and with another device of the ingenious Mr Quan, which even Colonel Yolland had seen fit to commend. This, which might if more widely known have been called in the terminology of the period 'Quan's Improved Patent Point Position Indicator', was a method of showing the position of facing siding points in relation to the main line. Briefly, the points were worked by a lever near the end of which was a round block of wood. Behind the lever was a post on which was a red-painted disc. If the points were set correctly, this disc was concealed by the block on the point lever. If they were wrongly set, the red danger sign was revealed. What happened at night is not recorded.

It was hoped to have the line open for passenger traffic by 1 October, but Colonel Yolland did not re-inspect it until 9 November, he was then sufficiently appeased to give it his (cautious) blessing. He found the line 'now in fair order', but was much exercised over the continued failure to provide toilets at intermediate stations. Nevertheless, when Marshall and Mr Page (the engineer) assured him that this would be attended to—a promise conveniently forgotten—he sanctioned the opening of the line to passengers on the following conditions:

(i) One engine in steam only
(ii) A maximum speed limit of 10 mph because of sharp curves
(iii) All locomotives to be at least six-wheeled and with a laden weight of not more than 13 tons (by a surprising coincidence this specification exactly fitted the existing machines!)

Whereupon the company lost little time in opening the line to passengers with the usual *éclat* and fuss.

The inaugural train, the 8.35 am ex-Ravenglass on 20 November, was given a formal send-off by none other than Lord Muncaster, who then rode on the engine to Boot which was reached at 9.20. The district, according to the local press:

> Was quite *en fête* over the event, flags being displayed at Ravenglass and various places along the line. In one instance—that of Mr Vicars, Gillbank—the flag was hoisted on top of a high crag known as 'The Burrows'.

And so, with a record goods tonnage for the year of 10,302 and a promising passenger traffic, the R & E got off to a fine start. As in the preceding May a coasting schooner had even loaded a cargo of iron ore on Ravenglass beach, there was yet hope of the harbour branch being built, but pride goes before a fall and, before 1877 was out, the R & E had fallen heavily.

CHAPTER 2

A Chequered History

IN CHANCERY

Scarcely had the railway opened for passengers than it was in danger of being closed again. The contractor discovered that, shares or no shares, the company owed him some £17,000 which it could not pay, and he thereupon sued it for the amount, confident of being granted possession of the physical plant in lieu of cash. The other major shareholder, Whitehaven Iron Mines Limited, which had promoted the line mainly for its own purposes and which had invested some £12,000 in it in various ways, was alarmed at the thought of losing its lifeline and, backed by other creditors, promptly put in a petition to the High Court of Chancery. The petition was heard before Vice-Chancellor Malins on 8 May 1877, and a provisional Order in Chancery was placed on the line on the 11th, being confirmed at the beginning of July 1877 by the appointment of a manager and receiver to control the line on behalf of its creditors.

Somewhat surprisingly, the 'proper person' chosen for this post was the R & E's then secretary, Henry Copland, who discharged his duty conscientiously for the next ten years. Meanwhile, the panic temporarily over, the railway settled down to its business of providing transport. Naturally enough, no fresh funds were available, except any excess of revenue over expenditure. The ingenius Mr Quan therefore used local resources to produce some additional wooden-bodied ore wagons and a peculiar coaching stock vehicle known as 'the big saloon'.

This, which can be clearly seen on page 36, resembled a cattle truck and was intended mainly for use at peak periods. Quan related later that on one occasion it had contained 100 passengers, which seems somewhat excessive! Quan himself remained 'manager' in spite of the official 'manager and receiver';

in reality, he and his successors would more correctly have been termed operating superintendents.

For the next two years, the railway worked uneventfully, carrying an average of about 15,000 passengers yearly but with steadily-declining mineral traffic as the Nab Gill lodes grew more difficult to work and the price of ore fell. App. 3 shows the struggle to produce a reasonable tonnage which, in most years, did not even cover working expenses.

THE GILL FORCE BRANCH

In 1880, a new source of traffic came to the railway. A civil engineer named William Donaldson and one James Allport, son of the Midland Railway's general manager, formed a concern called the South Cumberland Iron Company, of Boot, to prospect for iron ore both on Lord Leconfield's land higher up the valley by Christcliff farm (OS Ref 185012) and on the south side near Underbank (OS 176000).

These latter mines, at a location on the south bank of the River Esk known as Gill Force (not Foss as often printed), began work early in 1880, and a tramway of uncertain gauge was laid across farmland to the present Dalegarth terminus of the R & E.

The whole history of this branch is obscure but, in June 1880, Donaldson was having long and acrimonious discussions with the parish council about whether he could put in a level crossing over the main road or would have to build a bridge. His application for a crossing was strongly supported by Mr Quan and was approved towards the end of June—it would appear that a 3 ft gauge line was then laid in for, in July, an agreement was signed with the R & E to enable traffic to be passed on to that railway by a junction near Dalegarth Cottages.

The actual agreement is lost but, from various references, the authorisation was for a simple junction. There are persistent local recollections that the 3 ft gauge ran right up to the river at Underbank and it is likely that steam locomotives worked the tramway as a siding. Whatever the exact layout at Underbank, there was certainly more than one track so this would have been technically feasible. References in Leconfield papers previously thought to describe this section, however, turn out to refer to the Christcliff incline—the 'gig road'. The 41¼ lb/yd rail mentioned also explains why later it could be used to patch the R & E R main line (see p. 31). It is likely that the loading stage mentioned—a small affair, for it included only 127 lineal feet of timber—was for ore coming down by road from the Christcliff mine.

The layout at Underbank is equally in doubt, the relevant maps showing it as terminating in sidings at the mine mouth with a loop just before the river bridge. The girders of the latter are certainly quite substantial enough to support 3 ft gauge track but, from inspection of the site, it is probable that the 3 ft gauge terminated at a transfer point by the loop and that the 2 ft gauge mine bogies ran to that point (2 ft gauge was definitely used in the mines and, as they were adits, must have come at least to the surface). The loop site is liberally heaped with fragments of mined stone, supporting this theory, and it is notable that the impressive drystone walling enclosing much of the route right up to Dalegarth Junction is also of mined stone with traces of ore. It must have been a convenient method of disposing of ore spoil while at the same time fencing off the line.

Almost as soon as the 1880 agreement with Donaldson had been signed, the R & E was approached by another person wishing to use its services. This time it was one Edward Charter Maddison, a city banker whose son was prospecting for minerals in the district. Maddison wanted to lease the line lock, stock, and barrel for ten years with an option to buy it for £20,000, and a preliminary agreement to this effect was negotiated on 10 November 1880, subject to approval by the High Court of Chancery. Copland (the secretary of the R & E) went so far as to swear the necessary affidavit before a Commissioner for Oaths on 26 November, but apparently carried it no further—there is no record of Chancery proceedings, and the receiver's accounts for succeeding years show no trace of the annual rent of £1,000 stipulated. The agreement did contain a 'break clause' rendering it null and void if no action had been taken by 1 January 1881 and almost certainly was allowed to go by default.

Meanwhile, the railway carried on. 1880 and 1881 were peak years for goods traffic, some 11,615 tons and 9,004 tons respectively being carried, but the ore trade was declining rapidly and, in 1882 the inevitable happened; Whitehaven Iron Mines Limited failed, a petition for winding up the concern being filed on 20 March by 'various creditors and debenture holders'. A Mr J. H. Tilly was appointed as liquidator but does not seem to have hurried his duties for the company was not finally wound up until 1900.

The failure had immediate impact on the R & E, although ore shipments from the Nab Gill mines continued for a short while to fulfil existing contracts. Mr Quan left to seek his fortune in Australia and was replaced in mid-March 1882 by Mr Wilson Harrison, who lost no time in trying to cut down working expenses and—vainly—to stimulate traffic. He even wrote to Lord Leconfield's Estates suggesting the quarrying and sale of broken granite as the railway had just acquired a 'steam stone breaker'. Exactly what this machine was is not clear, but it was probably driven from the locomotives and used for crushing ballast. In any case, Leconfield's were not very encouraging and the matter was dropped.

Harrison no doubt had a very discouraging time during the next few years for work at Nab Gill was stopped altogether in the week ending 17 February 1883 and the railway was then dependent on traffic from Gill Force. This, after a brief peak of some 100 tons weekly in 1881, had declined to little more than that a month in 1883, the mines being abandoned altogether in late 1884. The main trouble was finance. An attempt was made to get capital by floating a limited company in 1882, but came to nothing. Furthermore, the Great and Little Barrow lodes at Christcliff had proved largely unproductive, only an insignificant annual tonnage of about 100 being won.

THE NAB GILL MINE CLOSES DOWN

The Nab Gill mine still had a small part to play in the railway's traffic, for a concern calling itself variously 'The Eskdale Mining Company, Boot', 'The Eskdale Haematite Iron & Mineral Company', or, occasionally, 'James Wingate & Company, Steamship Owners and Brokers', took a lease when Whitehaven Iron Mines withdrew and, after a short period, began to mine ore.

Leconfield Estate records show that some 1,275 tons were raised by September 1882 but, with prices ex-Ravenglass of only 8s 6d a ton, the railway did not benefit. Its charges were cut from 9d to 4d a ton in July, but the output from the mines dwindled to nothing. Instead, the mining company concentrated on extending the mine before giving up in disgust early in 1884.

In desperation, Harrison leased the mines himself for six months in 1884 from June to December, raising 1,400 tons of ore, but gave up at the end of the year, the mines then being virtually abandoned. Harrison himself stayed only another year as manager and, one gathers, was not universally popular. He is said to have negotiated the mail contract which began on 29 October 1888, and he also arranged for the locomotives to be repaired comparatively cheaply by the Furness Railway. In 1886, Harrison resigned, although he apparently maintained contact with the railway until he left the district nine years later. He was replaced by Sydney Woodley, a member of a prominent local family much interested in the railway. At the same time Henry Copland retired as manager and receiver, his place being taken by Mr (later Sir) Edward Moore, senior partner of a well-known London firm of chartered accountants, who was to retain the post until the end. Exactly why he was appointed receiver is not clear, but he proved a good friend to the railway and did his best to ensure its survival.

THE RAILWAY STRUGGLES ON

The history of the line over the next twenty years or so is one of make-do-and-mend against a background of local intrigue and ephemeral efforts to revive mineral traffic. The Leconfield Estates remained sceptical in face of several applications to operate Nab Gill mines in the 90's from various shaky organisations, and no work was done. Even Donaldson had a try in 1891, signing an agreement but then failing to take it up: he tried again in 1894, but was promptly told to go and develop his Stanley property (Gill Force) and then come back. Alas Gill Force was abandoned, and its tramway disappeared piecemeal as the farmers reclaimed the land across which it ran. Other applications from interested parties in 1896 and 1899 were also rejected.

There was hope of some granite quarrying. Messrs Ord & Maddison (son of E. C. Maddison) of 3 Northgate, Darlington, applied for a lease of the Beckfoot and Fisherground areas in 1887 and was granted a twenty-one year lease in spring 1888. Details are vague, but there is a reference in Leconfield records to 'the quarry at 200 ft elevation above Fisherground where young Mr Maddison made an impractical start.'

This effectively dates the opening of Fisherground Quarry, which was previously thought to have been initiated in 1910, and later references show that the incline and a siding from the R & E were also put in at this time. It is possible that some stone was also taken from Beckfoot for railway tonnages show a slight increase between 1888 and 1891, and it is obvious that little can have come from Fisherground.

Up until about 1900 the railway, then, was sustained only by some local goods traffic and an increasing number of tourists as the beauties of Eskdale became better known. Services varied between three and four trains each way daily, the last train running only as far as Beckfoot, an economy move which called forth occasional peevish grumbles in the local press.

There was undoubtedly a certain amount of intrigue going on behind the scenes for Donaldson, when he applied for the Nab Gill rights in 1894, hinted darkly at 'plots to ruin the little railway' and spoke of hoping to push a Bill through Parliament to restore the line's fortunes; while Tilly sold all the Whitehaven Iron Mines shares to Sydney Woodley's father Robert in 1892 for the princely sum of £150, an action which no doubt ensured Lewis Woodley's succession to the managership when brother Sydney left at the end of 1896 to take up a post on the Lancashire, Derbyshire & East Coast Railway.

Whatever plots there were certainly did not come from the railway's management nor, as has sometimes been implied, were the Woodleys behind whoever caused the deletion from the Furness Railway's 1899 Bill of the powers granted to buy or work the R & E. Indeed, they were obviously waiting in hope that the FR Bill would solve all their problems, for it was not until the amended Act had been passed that Sydney Woodley circulated the following rather interesting letter to his fellow creditors—the first of several attempts to revive the railway's fortunes (see page 30).

The two most interesting items are his points that, if Chancery charges were excluded, the operating surplus would be sufficient to cover debenture interest and, in the same breath, that presumably for lack of funds, no major repairs had been carried out to locomotives and stock since the line opened! The locomotives were normally attended to at Ravenglass shed by Furness fitters.

1900 must have been the nadir of the railway's traffic, with no granite or ore being carried and the evening service still restricted to Beckfoot. Fortunately, the tourists still came at weekends—the main trains on August Bank holiday that year required both locomotives double-heading all the coaching stock; but, the *Whitehaven News* recorded, 'prospects for the winter are not good'.

GRANITE WORKINGS

The only real ray of hope was that, in 1901, Bootle Council was allowed to take a certain amount of granite from a site near Beckfoot and this led to further prospecting by the firm of W. A. Fairbairn of Newcastle-on-Tyne. This concern began to probe on

PRIVATE AND CONFIDENTIAL.

From L. W. Woodley with Mr [illegible] 21/12/00 [illegible]

"VENTNOR,"
AVONDALE ROAD,
CHESTERFIELD,
December 8th, 1900.

DEAR SIR MADAM,

RAVENGLASS AND ESKDALE RAILWAY.

As a Bondholder in the above Railway, I beg to address the Creditors and Bondholders on the Company's position.

As you will be aware the Railway was opened for Traffic in 1876, and the Rolling Stock was built in that and the previous year.

I was in the Company's service for 18 years, and of this was 10½ years Manager, and am, therefore, in a position to give you the following from my own knowledge.

Since 1876 the Engines and Rolling Stock have been running regularly and without any extensive repairs, it will be evident therefore to you, that the time has come when a considerable sum of money must be expended in absolutely necessary repair.

From 1886 the receipts have steadily increased and there has been a considerable surplus each year after the ordinary working expenses have been paid, but the Chancery charges absorb a considerable amount of this surplus, and is a charge on our property, which if we can devise a reasonable scheme of re-arrangement, can be done away with and the money used for its legitimate purposes.

Last year the Furness Co. had a clause in their Bill to obtain powers to buy or work our property (an arrangement which would have been highly beneficial to us), but for some unknown reason the clause was dropped. It is evident, therefore, we must make some effort ourselves to release the property from the control of Chancery.

I have carefully thought the matter over and suggest for your consideration the formation of a new Company, and going to Parliament for Powers to purchase the existing Company's interest, the New Company's Capital to be £10,000, and issued and used as follows:—

£2,500	Three per cent. Debenture.	
	Holders of the existing Bonds and the Creditors to receive new at the rate of 2/6 in the £, which would absorb	£2,080
	And the remainder be issued to public	£420
£7,500	Ordinary Shares of £10 each.	
	New Shares at the rate of 1/- in the £ to be allotted to holders of existing Ordinary Shares, would absorb about	£1,100
	The remainder to be issued to the public, and be available for cost of obtaining Powers and for the improvement of present Rolling Stock and Railway, and providing New Stock	£6,400
£10,000		£10,000

The surplus after paying ordinary working expenses for the last 10 years has been more than sufficient to pay the interest on the proposed £2,500 3% Debentures, so that instead of being, as now, an unsaleable item, it would immediately become a dividend paying bond: with additional rolling stock, which the surplus capital would provide, the receipts would be further increased, and I consider the Ordinary Shares would also earn a dividend in a short time.

I should be glad to hear whether you approve a scheme on this basis being worked and if so, would you be willing to attend a meeting of the Creditors and Bondholders at some convenient centre, to fully discuss the matter. I may add that if accepted by the Creditors and Bondholders, I can obtain assent from holders of at least three-quarters of the existing Ordinary Shares, and from private enquiries I have made, I believe the £6,820 capital to be issued could be placed at par in the district the Railway serves.

Yours faithfully,

SYDNEY WOODLEY.

(2) *Sydney Woodley's letter to bondholders, December* 1900

Muncaster Fell in 1903 but found nothing suitable so began to negotiate with Leconfield Estates for a lease of the Beckfoot area.

All negotiations were done through a Mr J. J. Robson, 'Tramway Contractor and Dealer in Stone (Newcastle Electric Tramway—Western Extension)'. He took over the lease when it was signed at the end of 1904 and lost no time in beginning work. According to the local press late in December, a start had been made and men were 'busily removing the tramway rails formerly belonging to the old South Cumberland Iron Company from Underbank'—presumably the mine tramways, as much of the Gill Force line had by this time been reclaimed by farmers.

There was a precedent for this casual cannibalisation; a Mr Dixon Sharpe, when building the Stanley Ghyll Hotel in the 90s, had absentmindedly purloined part of the Nab Gill incline without telling anyone, but had been found out. The habit was obviously catching for, in 1905, the R & E paid Leconfield 50s a ton for the rails from Christcliff Incline—the main line must have been in an awful state if light quarry rail was being used to patch it!

To return to Mr Robson: the *Whitehaven News* reported on 9 February 1905 that:

> The granite Quarries at Eskdale and Muncaster have now got fairly to work. The granite near to Beckfoot is proving to be of very fine quality. Sidings are about to be connected with the R & ER and it is reported that more men will shortly be engaged.

It is not certain where the 'Muncaster' quarry was, although it must have been somewhere on the Fell. It may have been on or near the site of the later Murthwaite West quarry proposals.

Initial results were not promising despite the newspaper forecasts, no stone being sent away before the end of March when Robson was negotiating for a lease of Fisherground in the hope that it would be more suitable for sett-making. By the end of September 1905, he had sent away only 67 tons of broken stone, but a reasonable working face probably had been exposed by then as he was able to begin sending setts away on 6 November. Meanwhile he had applied to buy the brake wheel from Boot incline to let wagons down the Fisherground track but presumably did not do so as it is still at the foot of Boot incline; the wheel still dumped near Fisherground is that from the old Ban Garth mine.

There is no indication that Robson ever worked Fisherground, although Beckfoot was worked on a small scale for the next three years. It never generated enough traffic materially to help the R & E, by now in a parlous state and drawing less and less space in the columns of the local press.

THE R & E IN DECLINE

Mary C. Fair, the well-known local historian, has left a vivid account of the railway at this period in an article she wrote for the *Wide World* of 19 December 1903, from which the following extract is taken.

> The roads are awe-inspiring in their steepness, but there is...a still more surprising railway. North of Barrow-in-Furness is a junction called Ravenglass. "Change here for the Eskdale line," calls the porter. As your ticket is for Irton Road on that line you dismount and look around for your train. The porter collects your goods and, stepping across the rails past a goods shed, leads you to a tiny siding whereby is a tar-coated wooden shed, covering some extremely crookedly-laid rails, three feet in gauge. On the rails are an engine of primitive design, a van ditto, and one coach still more so. The coach is a "Composite" one, containing a guard's box, one third "smoker" and an ordinary third. These carriages hold at a pinch four slim adults-a-side, and are innocent alike of racks, cushions or communication-cords. As, however, the pace never exceeds five miles per hour, nervous passengers need not be deterred from journeying on the line on this account, for it is quite within the bounds of safety to alight while the train is going at full speed. Behind these vehicles, but not coupled to them is another passenger coach, containing a first-class carriage—the Royal saloon, so to speak. Tonight this is left behind to ease the engine's burden.
>
> There are no porters visible, but presently a guard arrives, and the engine, which has been employing its leisure in giving rides to two small boys, is coupled on ahead, and the guard, a composite official, unlocks a cupboard in the dim recesses of the shed and doles out four third-class tickets to the three others and yourself who comprise his load. He then locks up his "ticket office" and, packing you in, starts his tiny train on its perilous career up the valley. It lurches, and groans, and rolls along in a manner that makes you wonder why you did not invest your spare coppers in insurance tickets. You also speculate whether the bottom will fall out of the carriage, the train pull up the rails, or the whole affair topple over into the river.
>
> Thick bracken brushes the footboards at either side, from out of which the head of an ancient Herdwick ram gazes up at the snorting, labouring engine. It is evidently an old acquaintance, and he pays but little heed to it. The stoker, whistling cheerfully, sits on the cab, swinging one leg over the side with an airy grace all his own. Presently with a dislocating jerk, the train pauses dead with

> an abruptness that lands your portmanteau on your toes, and the stoker descends leisurely to drive a misguided ewe and lamb off the track into the clustering bracken. This act of mercy being accomplished, and a pedestrian who suddenly appears over a wall having climbed on board for a "lift", this weird express grunts its toilsome way at last into "Irton Road Station", a wooden hut with a siding whereon reposes a decaying truck filled with bricks. Here you dismount, and the guard, who has unlocked the hut and doled out more tickets, starts his comic-opera collection of relics off again on its uncertain way round a bend, up into the beautiful cleft among the hills where, several stations away, lies the terminus, which is known as Boot.

The state of the railway is evident from this lively account and it is from this period of its history that most of the apocryphal and semi-apocryphal stories of the line arise. Mary Fair herself relates how a local who wanted to buy a horse from a farmer, took the train to near the farm and requested the guard to pick him up on the return journey.

> That official accordingly stopped the train opposite the field where the price of the steed was still being hotly argued, waited until a bargain was struck and then hoisted the buyer on board the express.

The line was full of such courtesies, although it is recorded that, when on one occasion an individual stopped the train merely to ask the time of day, this was felt to be encroaching too much on the conveniences of the line and he was requested not to do it again!

Many of the stories one has heard as variations in umpteen minor railway sagas. Inevitably the dalesfolk used to walk along the track and inevitably on one occasion the train overtook an aged daleswoman going to market who, on being invited to join the train, tersely replied 'Nay, Ah's in a hurry. Ah can't be boddard wid you lot'.

More personal to the 'Ratty' are the guard who, when the big saloon's door jammed once, simply kicked it in, and the farmer's boy who, on being sent to collect a chicken coop, is said to have taken Eskdale Green Station by mistake. Certainly authentic is W. T. Palmer's account of a minor feud caused by a race from Eskdale Green to Beckfoot...

> It was a favourite trick of the bloods to pit some athlete against the train along this level. This considerably annoyed the driver,

> and to keep ahead he cut out the water stop. Usually the walker started when the train was heard to puff through the road bridge above the King George (then the King of Prussia) and somebody 'giving mouth' warned Jack of the contest (this would be old Jack Ashburner).
>
> 'I beat him by waiting until the train was past the inn door. The engineer threw bits of coal and some objurgations but I got to Beckfoot Station first. Jack paid me out when I took a gun to an Eskdale friend. He professed interest, produced a pair of cartridges, suggested that rabbits alongside the line were "tantalising".'
>
> At one point he shut off steam, and the train came down with less than the usual oscillation to where many rabbits were feeding. 'I fired right and left. Then Jack immediately put on all steam so that I should not pick them up. He did this himself on the return journey and so got level with me.'

It is quite obvious that, by 1904–5, the railway was more like one of the fancier Emmett creations than a working transport system and it must have been about the same period that *Nab Gill* finally expired as a working locomotive. Indeed, Mary Fair mentions the 'solitary locomotive' in her article but the 9.30 am train on August Bank Holiday 1904 comprised both locomotives and all the stock plus some wagons, so either a locomotive was away for repairs or lurking in the shed during her visit.

Certainly when, on Monday, 10 March 1905, the 9.35 to Boot was de-railed near Murthwaite by a broken fishplate, there is no record of the service being interrupted; although the locomotive finished up on its side against the bank and was off for several weeks getting thoroughly overhauled. On that August Bank Holiday, only one locomotive was steamable as, when it broke down, the service *was* interrupted until 'Mr Thomas and one or two others from Workington put it right later in the day.' It is likely that *Nab Gill* was very much on its last legs and only steamed as a last resort, and this is supported by the fact that all late vintage photographs show *Devon*.

Although the railway, too, was on its last legs, Lewis Woodley at least was still trying hard to get money for reconstruction. In January 1904 he sent a persuasive letter to the Leconfield agent urging him to buy up the outstanding debts (offered by the creditors at a fabulous discount!) and saying that Lord Muncaster had promised to donate his interest in the company in support of any claims—as he might well do, seeing it was worthless to him in any case!

This touching appeal fell on stony ground, and it was not until three years later that a really serious attempt to revive the line

Page 35: UP THE LINE – 2

[*above*] *The Stanley Ghyll hotel with a Ravenglass-bound short train consisting of 'Nab Gill' and the 3rd class coach.* [*below*] *A passenger train entering Beckfoot station*

Page 36: ASPECTS OF THE RAILWAY

[above] The train posed at the bottom end of Boot station, with the village behind. Note abscence of brake van. [below] Former 1st *class coach (now composite) and 'big saloon' Photograph taken about* 1907

got under way. This time it was headed by that conscientious man Edward Moore, who summoned 'those interested in the preservation of this Railway' to a meeting at Carnforth on 16 November 1907 and thus began a new and even odder chapter in the line's chequered history.

CHAPTER 3

The Eskdale Railway

ATTEMPTS AT REVIVAL

When Edward Moore called his meeting, the prospects for any restoration were unpromising. By the middle of 1908, when the first practical steps were taken, the railway was in a very sorry state. Earnings in the previous two years had not even covered bare working expenses, *Nab Gill* was unserviceable and probably partly cannibalised, the wagon stock was down to under twenty usable vehicles, while the coaches were falling to pieces (in fact a maker's plate did fall off one and was recovered from Ravenglass platform during reconstruction operations in 1966!). Despite a record crowd at Whitsun, which as usual overtaxed the line's capacity, receipts were in general declining and, with the track really unsafe for passenger working, the future was bleak. It is a mystery to the present writer how the ageing *Devon* ever managed to stagger up the valley that bank holiday, towing as she was not only all the coaching stock but also four packed wagons!

At this juncture, a number of people were persuaded by Moore and Woodley to support a scheme for re-building the railway primarily to carry passengers, and a prospectus based on an estimate of what would be needed to restore the line was accordingly published in the *Whitehaven News* of Thursday, 23 July 1908. It began imposingly:

> RAVENGLASS AND ESKDALE RAILWAY. PROPOSED SCHEME OF REORGANISATION. So many people are concerned in the existence of the R & ER which is vital to the prosperity of the district, it seems that it will be of general public interest to know what is being done towards reconstruction. A provisional scheme has been prepared, which after consideration of all circumstances, seems the most practical to meet the approval of the Court of Chancery, to which the scheme is to be submitted

> in due course. The larger the measure of support that can be given to the proposals in the meantime the better. The following relates what is proposed...

The prospectus then went on to detail the history of the line (erroneously giving the impression that Whitehaven Iron Mines had failed in 1877, thus causing the company's receivership and confusing future historians!). It pointed out that the existing rolling-stock was so unsuitable for tourist traffic that little attempt had been made to encourage it although it had been obvious for some years that the Dale as a whole would benefit greatly from easier access. It continued, glowingly:

> An estimate has been prepared by the manager of the line for the necessary expenditure for the relaying of about four miles of track with new steel rails of 45 lbs per yard and to re-sleeper with creosoted sleepers, to provide three new passenger coaches and an additional locomotive at a cost of about £6,000, and certain monies are required to repay advances and the costs of Chancery proceedings, and to put an end thereto, and thus enable the Company with a new Board of Directors to resume control. It is now therefore proposed to issue first mortgage debenture stock to the extent of £8000 being a first charge upon the railway and its equipment, and bearing interest at the rate of 7 per cent per annum. The claims under the foregoing money bonds and other creditors which have been established according to the Master's Certificate amount to £16,640, and it is proposed to issue preferred ordinary shares of £1 each paying 5 per cent in settlement of these claims...

Here the prospectus detailed how claims would be met and commended the debentures for subscription by those who were interested in the preservation of the line, creditors, and the investing public, promising to pay off the debentures within twenty-five years by a sinking fund.

As was quite common in such cases, the expected local support proved to be illusory. At a public meeting in Whitehaven a few weeks later, it was only by personal contributions from two well-known local sympathisers, Edward Bousefield Dawson and John Hell, supported by a further contribution of £500 from Lewis Woodley himself, that sufficient funds were raised to proceed with a Parliamentary Bill to form a new company. Those interested were heartened by Mr Edward Moore, the receiver, who not only offered to contribute to any new company which might be formed but also to pilot the Bill through Parliament, which he did at a cost of some £600 to himself. It was therefore decided to proceed with the formation of a new company to be called the Eskdale Railway Company.

THE ESKDALE RAILWAY BILL

A Bill was proposed late in 1908 to 'incorporate the Eskdale Railway Company and for vesting in the Company the undertaking of the Ravenglass and Eskdale Railway Company and for other purposes.' Its main purpose was to release the line from Chancery and to put the promoters in a position to control operations. The directors were named as Edward Bousefield Dawson, Simon Leeder, John Musgrave, and John Vicars. They were specifically empowered to convert the line to electric traction, some fairly complicated provisions safe-guarding the 'Postmaster General's electrical telegraphy' apparatus from any electrical disturbances which might, it was thought, arise from the proximity of overhead lines. It must be remembered that electric traction was still in its infancy in this country and that the company was being fairly bold in proposing its use. It is probable that Dawson was the leader in this enterprise: as a prominent resident of Lancaster, he would no doubt be well-informed on the then recently-completed Morecambe branch electrification.

The Bill also laid down procedures for at least partly satisfying the creditors of the old company and for providing borrowing powers for the new one. Among the provisions was a clause that the first charge on any monies raised would be the repayment of amounts owing to Edward Moore, but these were still outstanding in 1924! It would appear from the Bill and from notes in the local press that, although no shares were actually issued, interested parties had subscribed sufficient funds to make at least some attempt at rejuvenating the railway if the Bill were passed. A final prudent shot, incidentally, was a clause forbidding the company to resume passenger traffic before the line had been reconstructed and inspected in accordance with the Regulation of Railways Acts 1842 and 1871.

In the meantime, lack of funds caused the closure of the railway to all traffic from 30 November 1908, and the closure of the line in turn resulted in cessation of granite-quarrying at Beckfoot. It was devoutly hoped by the Eskdale Railway Company promoters that lack of a railway would quickly show local residents that they should support the new scheme.

ROBSON'S LEASE

Edward Moore was a very conscientious man and had no intention of letting the railway lie idle during the months that must elapse before the Bill became law. Fortunately, the Eskdale Mining Company resuscitated itself, beginning exploratory work in April 1909 at the old Nab Gill mines. A daily train 'for minerals, goods, parcels etc' was run from 24 May on and, in June, the proprietor of the Eskdale Quarries, John Joshua Robson, agreed to lease the railway for six months at a rent of £1,000 per annum to carry his quarry's products.

The lease is a fascinating document which, besides guaranteeing the receiver against any failure of plant or permanent way, included the hopeful proviso that, if anything did wear out or break, it must be replaced by new material which would then become railway property! Of even greater interest was the stipulation that passengers were not to be carried, although Robson could contract to carry minerals and general merchandise as well as his own products. A detailed schedule of rolling-stock that he could use was included, being 'one locomotive engine (*Devon*); eleven goods waggons (sic); one goods brake van.' It will be noted that the passenger vehicles were specifically excluded and the *Nab Gill* is not mentioned. In the author's opinion this does not necessarily indicate that it was no longer in existence. Two locomotives are mentioned in the annual returns up to 1908 and the very mention of *Devon* would have been unnecessary if only *Devon* had been in existence. It is more likely that *Nab Gill* was in the shed but unserviceable and quite possibly cannibalised to keep *Devon* running.

At about this time, too, another fascinating bit of history crops up which one might almost style in Edwardian fashion 'The Mysterious Affair at Fisherground Quarry.' For there was apparently another attempt at granite-quarrying above Fisherground farm in 1909-10, although local tradition has it that work did not proceed after the first blast. One old inhabitant, now dead, clearly recollected the siding points to the R & E being put in 'somewhere about 1910' and, up on the quarry floor, the top of a very solid tipping wagon is still rotting away in the undergrowth. It is probable that only an exploratory blast was made and work was discontinued when the stone was found to be unsuitable.

THE ESKDALE RAILWAY CO TAKES OVER

At Beckfoot Quarry, Mr Robson began operations in July, amending the service to a thrice-weekly train and operating this right up to the expiration of his lease at the year's end. In the meantime, the Eskdale Railway Bill had passed through all its stages and received Royal Assent on 16 August 1909. In spite of the lack of financial response, the directors of the new company met late in December and decided to try and keep the railway running while they raised funds for its reconstruction. The financial situation was somewhat involved as no shares had been issued and no repayments made to creditors of the old company, but it would seem that the passing of the Eskdale Railway Act automatically removed the line from Chancery and so the Eskdale Railway Company was a viable organisation until somebody bothered to take it to court. Certainly Mr Moore faded out of the picture, retiring as receiver while the new board of directors took over.

Lewis Woodley also retired, probably when Robson took over, and the new company appointed Mr Lewis Hastwell of Whitehaven as manager with effect from 1 January 1910. It was decided to continue the thrice-weekly goods trains 'until the track is relaid' although, according to the returns for the year, only one locomotive and eight wagons were still serviceable.

The operation was not a financial success, partly perhaps because Hastwell was ill for some time during the summer. Receipts did not even cover costs, although the Nab Gill mines were flourishing and during the autumn needed a daily train; this may be a reflection of the poor condition of the rolling-stock rather than of an upsurge of traffic! The company was forced to suspend all traffic on 1 November and the mines, although 'going well, with plenty of good ore, with 16 working and more being put in' had perforce to stop work on the 18th after the customary fortnight's notice. Mr Hastwell retired at the end of the year and it seemed that the railway was closed for good.

All was not yet lost, however; the mining company, rather a ramshackle concern in many ways, keenly felt the lack of a railway, and initiated negotiations with the Eskdale company's chairman, Edward Dawson, for a lease of the line. 'Mr Main, the mining company's engineer', as the *Whitehaven News* stated hopefully on 16 March, 'is even hoping for passenger traffic.' If he was, his dreams were soon dispelled by an inspection of the line!

None the less, the mining company decided to proceed and, perhaps in anticipation, work also re-commenced at the granite quarries at the end of March. The Eskdale Mining Company had negotiated a twenty year lease on Nab Gill mines and accordingly leased the railway for the same period from 10 April 1911 on similar terms to those which Robson had enjoyed. The lease was negotiated between Dawson and Edward Swan as chairmen of their respective companies and rent was fixed, realistically, at £50 per annum plus a proportion of the profits 'if applicable'. Once more *Devon*, eleven wagons and the brake van were the stock specified and the carriages, stored at Ravenglass, were specifically excluded although from press reports at least one was used to carry workmen.

The first train ran just after Easter, Mr Hastwell being reinstated as manager, and it was decided to provide a thrice-weekly service for general traffic, a proclamation to that effect being inserted in the *Whitehaven News* for 20 April 1911. The granite quarries sent sample setts to Goole and received an order for 50 tons; the mines re-opened on 15 May and were soon 'going well', and there were the usual hopes of a full-scale revival. These were slightly diminished by an unexplained shut-down at the mines in July and finally dashed by stormy weather early in November which blew over one of the old stations, probably Eskdale Green, and forced the mines to close on 3rd November because of flooding. Reading between the lines, it seems that the mining company was always in financial difficulties, keeping safety precautions to a minimum, and the men struck in July because of the dangers involved. The stoppage may, however, have been a side effect of a national coal strike which cut off supplies for the pumping engine.

The railway continued running for some time to bring down stockpiled ore, one Ravenglass-bound train being de-railed on Saturday, 3 December between Boot and Beckfoot. The crew, consisting only of Lister and one of the Ashburners, was not able to re-rail it, so left, and the de-railed train was a 'curiosity' for sightseers from all over the dale on the following day. Interestingly, the train consisted of engine, two wagons 'with several tons of ore', a *carriage*, and a brake van, and it is probable that the crew were going too fast for the state of the track. Significantly, their normal procedure between taking the train up to Boot in the morning and returning in the evening was to 'drink themselves comfortable' at the Freemason's Arms (now the Burnmoor Inn).

THE END

The railway was still not quite finished. The mines were reopened at the beginning of May 1912, probably when the summer conditions dried them out, but were worked only on a small scale 'the majority of miners...having secured employment elsewhere during the strike.' The railway continued in use spasmodically to carry the ore away. Hastwell even offered against the terms of the lease to convey the Eskdale Choir down the dale on their annual outing but, perhaps not surprisingly, they refused and went by wagonette! The usual hopes of passenger traffic flickered now and then, raised for a time by the conversion of the old Stanley Ghyll Hotel, just by Beckfoot Station, into a CHA Guest House; but the mines flooded briefly again early in September and the end was not far off.

It came on Monday, 20 December 1912, when the miners arrived to find the lowest level flooded and water rising rapidly in the shaft. By this time, only the lowest level was being worked because of expense. The mining company had no funds left to drain the mine and it closed for good. The railway ran spasmodically during the winter, probably in the hope that the mines would reopen, but in spite of optimistic press predictions that 'there should be no trouble in making a good railway service in Eskdale and carrying it over the mountains to Keswick' nothing happened. On 30 April 1913 the railway closed and lay moribund.

Page 45: STATION SCENES

[*above*] *A packed train at Irton Road, showing ore tipping wagons in use as overflow accommodation.* [*below*] *Issuing tickets at Beckfoot. Note the elaborate slot machine, unusual in such a remote spot*

Page 46: EXCURSION TRAINS

[above] Heavily-loaded excursion, behind 'Devon', enters Irton Road on Whit Monday, 1906 *or* 1908. *[centre] Same train 'blowing up' at Eskdale Green. [below] Still, they got there; the arrival at Boot*

Page 47: THE DERELICTION PERIOD

The only clear pictures available of this period are those taken by R. Proctor Mitchell in 1915 and reproduced here from the original block since the prints have been lost. We apologise for the block defects which appear outweighed by the historical interest of the views [left to right, top to bottom] Ravenglass station; Beckfoot Station, looking toward Ravenglass; Muncaster Mill halt; Irton Road Station; Boot Station; The water tank near Fisherground

Page 48: ORIGINAL STOCK

[above] An early photograph showing 'Sans Pariel' with complete stock of the period including the seven Oslo coaches, Heywood coach and brakevan and three Heywood wagons. Note 3ft gauge siding. [below] Railhead at Muncaster Mill with a typical train. The brass lettering and the different patterns of end-screen can be seen, as can the peculiar garden awning. The ex-3ft gauge rails look in surprisingly good condition

CHAPTER 4

Revival 1915-19

UNEXPECTED REVIVAL

The derelict railway might well have slumbered on for years, or else succumbed to the drive for scrap metal caused by the first world war, had not a peculiar series of events taken place which resulted in its complete rebirth on the far narrower gauge of 15 in.

This last fact alone was surprising enough for, despite the advocacy of Sir Arthur Heywood at the end of the nineteenth century, no lengthy lines of such a narrow gauge had previously been built. For this secluded line to be discovered by a group of men who wanted to run 15 in gauge railways for pleasure—and in the midst of war at that—was even more unlikely, but in fact is what took place.

The story really begins some ten years previously when a miniature railway enthusiast by the name of Robert Proctor Mitchell began to run 15 in gauge pleasure lines at seaside resorts, notably at Southport and Rhyl, in some form of collaboration with the then still-to-become famous model engineer W. J. Bassett-Lowke. The enterprise was operated under the name of 'Narrow-Gauge Railways' and gradually extended its enterprises to include the running of exhibition lines abroad, although these appear to have been financed and equipped almost entirely by Bassett-Lowke, by then a firm specialising in miniature railway equipment. In the years immediately preceding 1914, lines were operated at Brussels, Lyons, Geneva, and Christiania (Oslo), and various items of equipment were exchanged between these and other ventures of the same concern, a procedure no doubt very convenient for the promoters but one which has caused many a headache to the historian!

Meanwhile, in 1911, the co-operative venture had been regularised by the registration of Narrow Gauge Railways Limited, with a nominal capital of £100, Proctor Mitchell and Bassett-Lowke being named as the directors. The secretary was John Wills, who will reappear in our story later on.

When war broke out, Narrow Gauge Railways Limited found itself in difficulties. The leases on its seaside lines had run out and were not renewed and foreign exhibition work was sadly curtailed. Proctor Mitchell, who appears to have taken the most active part in organising operations, looked round for new sites on which to use the Bassett-Lowke equipment then lying idle. He somehow heard about the derelict Eskdale Railway and, early in 1915, paid a visit to the line to examine the prospects of using its trackbed.

To judge from the photographs he took Mitchell found desolation rampant. The old stock still stood in Ravenglass Station, weeds and even young trees encumbered the right-of-way, and the stations were in appalling disrepair. This did not matter, for all that was needed was the track and most of this could be re-used. The 3 ft gauge rails, although worn, were still quite sound enough in most places to support the weight of a 15 in gauge train, and even the sleepers, though rotted at the fastenings, were sound enough in the centre for the narrower gauge to be safely spiked down.

ODD AGREEMENTS

The first peculiar event now took place; Narrow Gauge Railways Limited began negotiations for a lease of the line with Edward Bousefield Dawson, the former chairman of the Eskdale Railway Board. Although Mitchell and Bassett-Lowke probably did not realise it at the time, this was all quite without any apparent authority, for Dawson was only one of several surviving creditors of the Eskdale Company and had no right whatsoever to dispose of any part of the railway—which was, in any case, an incorporated company heavily in debt and which had never applied for an Abandonment Order to allow it to give up its undertaking.

It is also unlikely that Dawson, a most prominent and respected resident of Lancaster—who had at one time even been chairman of Lancashire Quarter Sessions—would knowingly have engaged in criminal actions, so it would appear that he was unaware of the legal problems and possibly considered himself the sole surviving creditor. One would guess that, while no capital had been raised by the Eskdale company, Dawson himself had financed operations and saw in this arrangement a way of re-couping some of his losses. This explanation, however, does not account for the sum specifically mentioned in the 1909 Act as owing to Sir Edward Moore and never repaid.

Whatever the circumstances, Dawson clearly felt he had rights of negotiation. Without consulting anyone, he leased the line to NGR Limited for three years in the first instance and simply pocketed the proceeds. The original agreement, signed on 22 July 1915, is such an interesting document that the main clauses are worth quoting in full:

> It is hereby agreed as follows:
> 1. The said Edward Bousefield Dawson will lease to the said Company for the consideration hereafter mentioned THE SITE Lands Buildings Works and everything appertaining to the said Railway except the Locomotives and rolling stock for the term of THREE YEARS from the date aforesaid (22nd July) and will do all acts and deeds necessary for such leasing especially all acts and deeds necessary to enable the Company to work trains over the Lands over which the Trains ran and where the Lines or Permanent Way still remain and will guarantee the Company free use of such Lands without interference by any adjoining Landlord or Tenant.
> 2. THE said Company will alter the Lines to suit their usual Locomotives and Rolling Stock using the Lines and Sleepers as present laid as far as possible.
> 3. THE said Company will provide and instal such necessary Locomotives and Rolling Stock as they may think necessary for the said Traffic and will commence running at the earliest date possible.

The rental was to be half of the gross profits, whatever these might be!

It will be noted that the agreement specifically excludes the old locomotives and stock from the lease as they would be useless to the new operators and it appears that Dawson, again without any authorisation, promptly sold them for scrap. No clear details are available at this length of time about what must have been a very quietly-conducted event, but local recollections are that the locomotives were cut up and their remains taken away by rail; the coaches were sold to local farmers and removed by large road wagons, and the goods wagons were burned on the spot, presumably because they were cluttering up the yard. Whether or not this is true, some stock was certainly still in existence in late 1915 or early 1916, for early photographs of the 15 in gauge show vehicles parked on the old loading bank.

THE RAILWAY REOPENS

While all this negotiation was going on, the second peculiar event took place. NGR Limited did not wait for the agreement to be signed but, early in July, began work on re-laying the line, working from Ravenglass. This activity was the first intimation to local inhabitants that anything was happening, the *Whitehaven News* for 16 July remarking in a rather surprised manner:

> The news that a narrow gauge light railway is to be run up Eskdale and that it is already in course of construction is glad tidings for Eskdale.

The local gossips never caught up with what was going on and there were various over-optimistic prophecies that the new line would be open 'soon'. On 22 July it was 'confidently expected that on August 1st the new light railway will be running up the valley at all events as far as Irton Road' but on the 5th of that month it was not yet open 'as the rolling-stock has not arrived' and the paper, while still optimistic, was too engaged in dispelling 'wild visions of an electric line over Hardknott Pass' to give many details besides the inevitable reminiscences of 'the 3 ft'.

It was not until 28 August that the 15 in gauge was opened for traffic and then only as far as Muncaster Mill while, even by the end of the year, it had got no further than Irton Road (opened Oct 1915). At the end of the year, too, the registered office was changed to Ravenglass, nominal capital having been increased to £1,000, of which only two £1 shares had been issued—one to each of the directors. Equipment was initially supplied by Bassett-Lowke, finance being provided by revenue and by the issue of successive lots of debentures, some £2,380 having been raised in this way by mid-1917.

At this juncture it is perhaps time to refer to the early personnel and operation of the line. There is a confusing reference in the local press to the appointment as manager of one 'Harry Short, formerly of Polytechnic Tours' (a company with which Mitchell was associated) but, from available records, John Wills, the secretary, managed the line from the beginning. He personally drove the locomotive on important occasions and later, when further locomotives were acquired, was often seen driving a relief train. To help him in the early years he had several old Eskdale Railway employees including John Lister and one of the Ashburner brothers.

The rolling-stock initially consisted largely of Bassett-Lowke equipment made idle by the ending of other NGR enterprises. Accounts of the opening, together with early photographs, show it to have included the total stock from NGR's Oslo exhibition line, comprising one 4–4–2 'Little Giant' of Class '30', *Sans Pareil* (formerly *Prins Olaf*) and seven Bassett-Lowke four-wheeled open coaches, some of which had end-screens and light canvas awnings. There were also from the beginning what the *Whitehaven News* described as 'a closed first class coach and brake van' which were of obvious Heywood design. These, together with a small number of wagons and possibly the Heywood dining car, appear to have been acquired from Sir Arthur Heywood's Duffield Bank railway some little time before his death and it is likely that he was sufficiently interested in the project to provide this help.

In any case, the stock was very soon further augmented from various sources after the extension of the line to Eskdale Green on 27 March 1916, and to Beckfoot on 20 April of the same year, made the provision of more locomotives and stock vital: winter traffic was very light and could be handled by *Sans Pareil,* but a full summer service was quite a different matter!

In this situation the company was fortunate in finding several sources of stock ready to hand, and two locomotives were quickly brought up from the Duke of Westminster's estate railway at Eaton Hall. Only one was actually owned by that line, this being the famous—or infamous—0–4–0T *Katie,* finally rendered redundant at Eaton Hall by the acquisition of a new 0–6–0T. The other was at Eaton Hall only for trials, having been built in late 1913 for Captain J. E. P. Howey's new 15 in gauge estate line at Staughton Manor. It was Bassett-Lowke's first 15 in gauge Pacific, a straightforward elongation of the Class '30' 'Little Giant' and known alternatively as the '60' or 'Gigantic' class. Howey named it *John Anthony* but, when war broke out in August 1914, he went into the army and was taken prisoner, and the Staughton Manor line languished unused. In 1916, *John Anthony* was available for sale and promptly bought by NGR Limited for its new enterprise, being re-named *Colossus*—a name probably reflecting the flamboyance of Proctor Mitchell.

There is a mildly discreditable story about its acquisition which will probably bear repeating now that it will harm no one. It seems that, after the war, Captain Howey met Sir Aubrey Brocklebank, who chaffed him about the fairly high price of £800 which NGR had had to pay. Howey became most indignant about this, eventually disclosing that he had sold the locomotive to Mitchell for only £400, the latter apparently having made 100 per cent profit on the deal.

NEW BLOOD

Katie and *John Anthony* arrived for the 1916 season, possibly accompanied by some further Bassett-Lowke coaches intended for Staughton Manor. Photographs show modified vehicles with canvas tilt hoods of touring car pattern and doors to each compartment, and the line had a total of thirteen such coaches that year. They were soon followed by more stock, this time from Duffield Bank, the equipment of which had been sold by auction on 31 May 1916, following Sir Arthur Heywood's death. The complete story is not clear, but the equipment, comprising, besides rails, buildings, bridges, etc, almost the entire locomotive and carriage stock, was bought as a unit by a Derby firm which intended, so it is said, to use the two locomotives, 0–6–0T *Ella* and 0–8–0T *Muriel*. However, these and the rails were commandeered by the Ministry of Munitions for use in constructing the big ammunition depot near Gretna Green. Certainly, although they eventually reached Ravenglass in the summer of 1917, they came some time after the bulk of the Duffield Bank equipment which was apparently re-sold to NGR very soon after the auction.

The sale catalogue is extremely interesting as it tends to confirm both that Heywood had loaned or sold equipment to NGR Limited earlier, and that NGR Limited actually built a number of Heywood-type closed coaches (see p 146). Briefly, the stock included four bogie open coaches, the sleeping car, and a very few wagons, including various oddities, some of which also reached Ravenglass. There were *no* complete closed coaches, but a new one was listed as 'under construction' and this could well have been a replacement for the single coach supplied to NGR Limited in 1915—just as six brand-new four-wheel wagons were probably replacements for those which had already gone to Ravenglass.

The six wagons went to Eaton Hall, but the rest were welcomed by the hard-pressed R & E which was finding it difficult to cope with the traffic, even in the midst of a war. They must have been very hard-pressed indeed, for even *Katie* had to be used regularly on relief trains having already put in some twenty years' hard work at Eaton Hall. She certainly gave rise to many jocular stories when she was pressed into use and gave John Wills some very frustrating moments. She was wont, as one visitor recalls, to proceed:

> in a series of short rushes punctuated by long periods of breakdown. During these halts, some of the passengers roamed the countryside picking heather or searching for bilberries or mushrooms; others watched fascinated as Mr Wills, the driver, wrestled with the refractory locomotive.

On this particular occasion over three hours was taken to get from Eskdale Green to Ravenglass but, in an almost Victorian spirit of self-education: 'the run was regarded by us all as a classic conquest by man over matter' and all passengers appear to have been highly edified by the occurrence.

TRIALS AND TRIBULATIONS

Katie was especially bad but, in general, the locomotive stock was found not wholly suitable for working such a difficult and extended road, particularly after, in April 1917, the passenger service was further extended up the stretch of 1 in 38 to the old Eskdale Railway Station at Boot. The scale models, although free-steaming, were too lightly built and not powerful enough for summer traffic, while the Heywoods, hampered by the inherent defects of their pinnace-type boilers, could not sustain the power needed for a seven-mile run over such difficult country. Nor was the motive power position helped by an obscure but undoubtedly monumental crack-up sometime in the summer of 1917 when both *Colossus* and *Sans Pareil* appear to have run very badly off the rails! No details survive, but photographs show them lying crumpled by the lineside and, later, running in a very jury-rigged condition without running plates and with the tender bodies on flat wagons—a circumstance which suggests that their absence was sorely felt.

The accident was certainly severe enough to warrant an extensive re-build, at least of *Colossus,* and there is no doubt that the locomotives were often pushed to the limit and subjected to very severe strain. Indeed, particularly at peak periods, trains often had to be double-headed and consisted of several portions run 'on sight'. The later ones were often made up of Heywood wagons with plank seats and entrusted to *Katie;* it was on these occasions that the Ratty tradition of passengers pushing on the steeper gradients was initiated.

It might be thought that, even so, the company could settle down to a period of consolidation but this was not to be. First, the long final pull up to Boot proved too much of a strain for the engines and, at the end of the 1918 summer season, the service had to be cut back to Beckfoot; then the railway, always shaky financially, suffered a managerial and financial crisis simultaneously when, in mid 1918, an acrimonious quarrel between Mitchell and Wills led to the dismissal of the latter and his suing the company for three months' wages in lieu of notice. This would almost certainly have ruined the R & E's finances but, the matter was more or less amicably settled. One suspects the mollifying hand of Bassett-Lowke as John Wills remained in NGR employ, while being transferred to another of its enterprises at Fairbourne. Here he was outside Mitchell's influence—and ironically soon found himself saddled with a legacy of his former job in the shape of *Katie*! At Ravenglass, Proctor Mitchell, always the practical director of the concern, took over the managership himself and perhaps the most happy-go-lucky period of the Ratty's eventful history began.

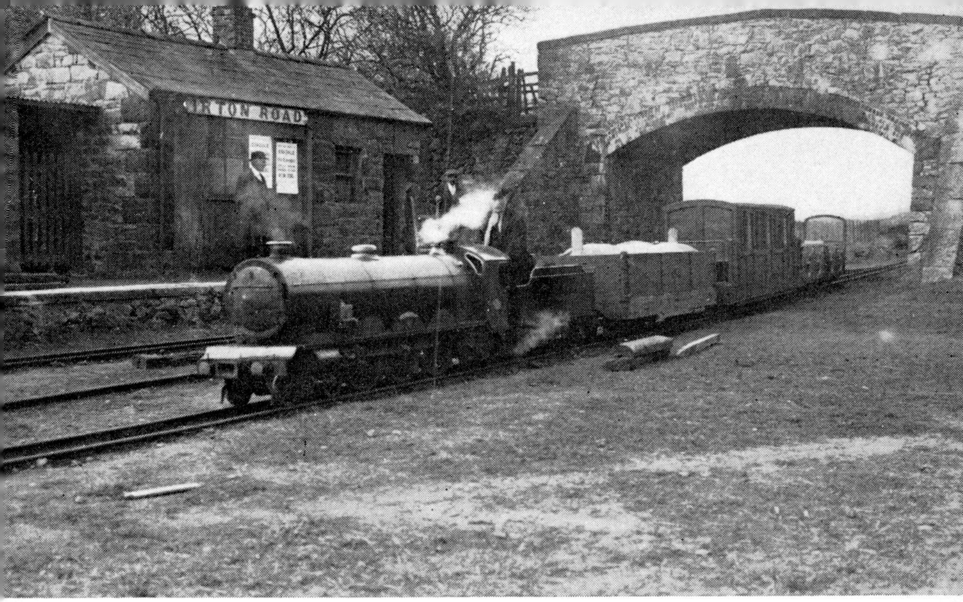

Page 57: FIRST REINFORCEMENTS

[*above*] *'Colossus' at Irton Road on a train including the Heywood 3 ton bogie wagon. The locomotive still carried the name 'John Anthony' and 'Staughton Manor Railway' on her tender.* [*below*] *Heywood 0–4–0T 'Katie' at Irton Road with Heywood stock 'standard' coach, flat wagons serving as bolsters, 3 ton bogie wagon, and four-wheel box wagons*

Page 58: UP THE TOP END

[*above*] *The two scale model pacifics, 'Sir Aubrey' leading 'Colossus' on the three-track layout at Dalegarth (new) station.* [*below*] *Proof that they got there: 'Muriel' and a train of Heywood stock in the old 3 ft gauge station at Boot*

CHAPTER 5

The Mitchell Era

THE AMATEUR PROFESSIONALS

Nowadays, we tend to think of amateur railwaymen as having grown up with the preservation societies, but the personnel of Narrow Gauge Railways Limited antedated these by many years. They can perhaps best be described as a bunch of professional amateurs, enthusiastic eccentrics—or vice versa—who had dabbled in miniature railways and who were now learning as they went the problems of operating a full-length railway over difficult terrain with very little financial backing!

The only money they had initially was that provided personally by W. J. Bassett-Lowke and R. Proctor Mitchell, together with revenue from the passenger traffic. This was not enough to keep pace with the wear-and-tear on equipment and, if it had not been for the benevolent interest and financial aid of a local resident, Sir Aubrey Brocklebank, the venture probably would have foundered in its first five years.

Sir Aubrey, then reigning head of the famous ship-owning family which later controlled the Cunard Line, lived at Irton Hall, some three miles inland from Ravenglass. He took a great interest in everything likely to benefit the district. He was early involved in the affairs of the R & E, providing capital in the form of debentures as early as 1917 and, in 1919, paying for the construction of a further scale-model 'Pacific' appropriately named *Sir Aubrey Brocklebank*. In 1918 he even got Mr Cecil J. Allen to survey a 15 in gauge branch from the R & E near Murthwaite to the grounds of Irton Hall. This was never built, although an entirely separate 15 in gauge line was used on part of his estate near Santon Bridge during the building of an estate dam.

There is no doubt that a businessman like Sir Aubrey, however benevolent his motives, must have felt some anxiety at the happy-go-lucky way the R & E was being operated as he could doubtless well imagine the quite substantial sums of money he had provided disappearing without trace. To understand his unease, it is perhaps appropriate at this point to take a look at the very mixed bunch which was operating the railway and, it is fair to say, in some cases playing at trains.

At the head of the permanent staff was R. Proctor Mitchell as general manager, 'the dominant personality of the period' as he was later described. Mitchell's history is obscure, but it was always understood on the line that his family was connected with ship-owning and that Mitchell himself came from a very wealthy background. Although the company documents described him as 'clerk' he was apparently a very experienced engineer, having served an apprenticeship with a firm of pump-makers and then done sea-time in ships connected with his family—or so it was said.

Mitchell came into railway work via the original NGR enterprises and was undoubtedly extremely valuable to the infant R & E which required engineering eccentricity most of the time! As a general manager he seems to have been technically capable but far too kind-hearted. Peter Le Neve Foster who, as a young engineer, worked under Mitchell, recalls that 'the old governor', as he was affectionately known, was always sympathetic to hard-luck stories and many of the casual employees on the railway were 'down-and-outs' to whom Mitchell was giving another chance in life.

Too often, these protégés took advantage of his generosity, and the railway company suffered in consequence. From this point of view, it was a pity that more practical interest in the line could not have been taken by W. J. Bassett-Lowke, a keen businessman if ever there was one, but he was too occupied with his flourishing model engineering business to do more than pay occasional flying visits. Indeed, apart from Mitchell himself, it was the summer immigrant workers and the various 'visiting consultants' to the line who provided most of the real eccentricity. The members of the permanent staff, although often flamboyant and unorthodox, supported Mitchell well, on the whole.

Perhaps the most important of the latter was the redoubtable Robert (Bob) Hardie, later known for his work on the R H & D. Hardie came in the very early days in 1916 with the grand title of superintendent of the line—although, as Le Neve Foster recalls, 'he was in fact nothing more nor less than a good working foreman'—but then the assumption of imposing 'main line' titles was almost an obsession among the NGR senior employees, especially the honorary consultants! Anyway, Bob Hardie is remembered with affection as a fair man and one who could always keep the passengers happy whatever occurred—a very valuable asset on the Eskdale line.

His background was vivid and varied. He had been associated with Mitchell in the Norwegian side of Polytechnic Tours and, before that, had run a barber's shop in London. Indeed, so it is said, he had once won the World Championship for quick shaving in Chicago, in 1903-4. A florid, genial man, he lived near Mitchell at Irton Road and, in his spare moments, kept hens in, of all places, the old Heywood brake van. He went to New Romney in late 1925 and was greatly missed.

Of the other permanent staff, some were local and some were imported. Perhaps the best bargain the railway got among these was Harry Hilton, who was one of Mitchell's better finds. His past was even more obscure than his master's, but there was a legend that he had once been private valet to Lord Rothermere. According to a contemporary, his jobs on the railway varied from 'pressing Mitchell's best trousers and typing the correspondence, to driving engines and doing other manual jobs'. A native of Kennington, he nevertheless settled down in Eskdale very well and stayed on the railway for the rest of his life. He ended it as general manager, a post he held up to 1959, and many readers of this book will doubtless remember his cheerful grin and helpful welcome to enthusiasts.

Of the rest there is not a great deal to say. They included at least one ex- Eskdale Railway man, John Lister; several members of the Lowther family, well-known local residents; and various others. Amongst them, fortunately, was Peter Le Neve Foster, a young apprentice engineer who, through Mitchell's kindness, was enabled to work on the railway for several summers and whose recollections of the staff are the basis for most of these notes. The fitters were a man named Johnson and, on occasion, John Lister, who could turn his hand to most things, but occasionally extra help was borrowed from the Furness Shops at Barrow...and Eskdale Railway history has a habit of repeating itself as Le Neve Foster recalled:

> ...the fitter (from Barrow) was a very funny little man and on Easter Monday he turned up on the railway as a passenger complete with his family and ordered a whole sheaf of privilege tickets. He was dressed in his Sunday best and he had an enormous

flower in his buttonhole and he was bringing his family for a trip up the line to show them the engines he had repaired. The engine, I think it was *Sir Aubrey Brocklebank,* didn't behave very well and I can still see that Furness Railway fitter jumping off the first coach at Ravenglass and rushing round behind the engine between the station and the Ravenglass shed trying to identify what the fault was.

THE 'CONSULTING ENGINEERS'

So much for the permanent staff and their eccentricities. One must additionally mention two at least of the 'visitors' who were in succession, entitled 'consulting engineers' to the railway. Just why the company ever needed a consultant is obscure as from all accounts Mitchell was a very fine practical engineer. Nevertheless, it had one.

His name was Cauchi—rudely changed by almost all employees behind his back to an unprintable piece of rhyming slang—and he is an even more obscure figure than the rest. He was definitely an amateur with private means and all the R & E staff ever knew of him was gleaned from his flying visits which were usually preceded by imperious telegrams demanding that a special train be kept in readiness for him in case he wanted to go up the line. He was supposed to have designed *Sir Aubrey,* though in practice this can have amounted to little more than a few modifications to the Greenly design, but all he is remembered for is an almost morbid fear of boiler explosions. He must have had many jittery moments from *Sans Pareil,* which normally worked his specials and which had a disconcerting habit of making too much steam far too easily when she was standing idle.

Cauchi was followed round about 1920 by Henry Greenly, a controversial figure whose idiosyncrasies will not be discussed here. As far as the R & E was concerned, he was a touchy but useful ally with a reputation for being charming to subordinates but awkward and quarrelsome with his equals and superiors. His association with the line began with a strong quarrel over the provision of working drawings to which he claimed the NGR had no right. There are several variants of this tale, but it seems likely that it arose when *Sir Aubrey* was being designed and drawings of *Colossus* were required. In any event, the matter was eventually smoothed over although not until the day before a threatened action was to be heard in the High Court. *Sans Pareil* drawings were eventually used, while Greenly became the company's consulting engineer. Whatever his faults, he was a very good designer, and the present *River Esk* is a lasting memorial to his hard work. It might serve, too, as a reminder that, however haphazard and eccentric they all were, without them British miniature railways would probably have died with Heywood and the R & E would certainly not have survived.

With them, and with Sir Aubrey's benevolent help, survive it did. Sir Aubrey was very soon called on once more after the Mitchell group had taken over as, despite the cutback in services to Beckfoot and the resulting easing of strain on motive power, the locomotives were causing anxiety. *Katie* in particular was almost completely worn out and was eventually disposed of during 1918 to the Llewellyn Miniature Railway at Southport and, reading between the lines, it would seem that *Muriel* was not in a much better state. Visitors to Ravenglass around the 1920 period rarely saw her in steam except on occasions of great stress, although *Ella* was apparently in frequent use.

MORE STOCK

It was decided to obtain a new locomotive, and the choice fell on another scale model, a slightly modified version of *Colossus*, appropriately named *Sir Aubrey Brocklebank*—there can be no doubt who paid for that! The chief differences were an increase in boiler diameter and in power, which took the dimensions outside the British scale loading gauge. The locomotive was built not by Bassett-Lowke, but by a firm called Hunts which had never built a locomotive before and has never built one since. Whatever the circumstances, which are discussed fully on pp 117-19, that firm turned out a good job and *Sir Aubrey* was the pride of the line for the next few years.

Stock, too, was in extremely short supply, especially during peak periods when anything that moved had to be pressed into service. Oddly enough, it seems that no attempt was made to re-build the Heywood 'oddities' which had accompanied the standard stock—ie the dining and sleeping cars, or the luggage van with end balconies. The first two mouldered away on trestles as stores at Ravenglass and Irton Road, and the luggage van disappeared to house Bob Hardie's chickens.

Instead, the line acquired a collection of 15 in gauge stock from Sir Robert Walker's Sand Hutton Estate in Yorkshire; his line was being converted to 18 in gauge and the stock was redundant. From this source the R & E received a rather odd bogie saloon, fully described on page 153, and, probably, four Bassett-Lowke four-wheel open coaches which no doubt would be used to reinforce the diminishing stock of originals. Rumours of an eight-wheel luggage van ex the SHR appear unfounded as the latter never had such a vehicle, and there may well be confusion with the obscure Heywood vehicle referred to above.

The saloon, which was a lightly-built but closed vehicle, proved especially useful for winter services. These had early proved uneconomic, but a contract for carriage of His Majesty's mails required such a service to be provided and the lighter the stock the cheaper the motive power required. The SHR coach was certainly more comfortable than the only other lightweight, a crudely-roofed Bassett-Lowke four-wheeler with windows only in the end. It was also light enough to be pulled by an internal combustion-engine 'device' and almost certainly called into existence the first of a series of ephemeral 'scooters'.

This was a simple four-wheel trolley on which was mounted a 'Wall Autowheel' two-stroke engine—the forerunner of moped engines. It lasted only long enough to perish in a head-on collision in 1921 with *Sans Pareil* when on a mission of urgency, but the principle was proved. *Sans Pareil* appeared for a time with a 'jury-rigged' tender, its body mounted on a wooden flat truck; and a succession of little two-strokes followed the Wall. An 'Economic' 2 hp machine lived and died briefly without attracting much attention; a little Douglas-powered 'thing' was at one time fitted with a windshield very like the motor scooters of today, but faded away before 1925, and, after the new régime took over, a Scott 'Flying Squirrel' engine was built into a peculiar box-like structure reminiscent of an early motor-car and gave the staff many exhilarating rides. The main incident of its career was an encounter en route with a furious horse which smashed the engine casing with one mighty kick. The breed did not die out until about 1930, by which time more solid petrol-engine machines had arrived, but they left their marks, often literally. One thing they all had in common was a lack of dignity.

Apart from the Scott, which boasted a kick-start, the universal method of starting was for the driver to sprint alongside until he judged sufficient speed had been attained and then to let in the clutch as he nimbly leaped into the saddle. What with the eccentricities of all these machines, Mitchell's permanent way staff must have been quite thankful when, in the winter of 1922-3, the first real petrol tractor appeared.

This was 'real' only in the sense of not being a home-concocted object. Otherwise, it was a wonderfully eccentric machine which fitted excellently into the Ravenglass atmosphere, a peculiar survival of the first world war. Known as a Crewe Tractor, from its unlikely conception by the London & North Western Railway's Crewe Works, it consisted of a Ford Model 'T' car chassis complete and mounted on a four-wheel truck which it drove by chain and sprocket from the rear axle. Soon embellished with a grotesque 'hut' strongly resembling an average family 'two-holer', it chugged serenely up and down the vale for several years before coming to an untimely end.

Yet amid this blaze of eccentricity, things got done. 1922 was the climactic year for the Mitchell régime. First, passenger services were once more extended up the Beckfoot bank and then round over part of the former Gill Force line in front of the old miners' cottages. The terminus was given the romantic-sounding name of Dalegarth and, from all accounts, some of the mineral branch was still *in situ* at the time, at least at that end. Photographs show re-laying to the 15 in gauge in progress.

Experiments were also made about this time with a slip portion on certain 'express' trains, for Irton Road passengers. This was more of a gimmick than anything else, although it did perhaps avoid stopping a heavy train at Irton Road, and never came to much. The scheme was operated on a small scale in 1922 and again in 1923 and the early part of the 1924 season, but was then discontinued.

GRANITE TRAFFIC AGAIN

The main event of 1922 was another venture by Sir Aubrey. In company with a group of local sett-makers he founded the Beckfoot Quarry Company with the intention both of providing employment in the valley and traffic for the railway. The old Beckfoot Quarry was opened up, new wagons were ordered, and Henry Greenly designed his masterpiece, the 2–8–2 *River Esk,* which came the following year from Davey Paxman to handle the heavy stone traffic.

Greenly also designed a beautiful model-engineering-style crushing plant to deal with the broken stone and this was built in 1924. To avoid marring the valley more than was absolutely necessary, it was situated away from anywhere under the towering north face of Muncaster Fell. Murthwaite, for so it was called after a neighbouring farm, does not see the sun at all for four months in the year, and it must have been a grim place to work in even when in full operation, but it brought new revenue to the railway which had not only to bring stone to it but also had to haul the crushed stone away to Ravenglass as the plant had no road access. To deal with this traffic, a rotary tipper was installed at Ravenglass on the site of the old 3 ft gauge tipping dock and, later on, about 1927, a steel chute was fixed by the railway bridge to enable the filling of road vehicles to be carried out as well.

The traffic from Beckfoot brought revenue; it almost certainly permitted the construction in 1923-4 of six four-wheel open coaches which were prefabricated at Barrow-in-Furness and assembled into their running gear at Irton Road, being carried there on flat wagons made of old Bassett-Lowke coach frames. It also brought problems until the *River Esk* arrived. The Heywoods took the brunt of the work, especially *Ella*, but they were ageing, and both *Colossus* and *Sir Aubrey* had to be used at times. Their adhesion proved insufficient under bad conditions, and both were fitted with big sandboxes forward of the buffer beams. *Colossus* had a temporary false extension buffer-beam bolted on to provide a platform for twin boxes, while *Sir Aubrey* acquired a tall tank-like box which rose above her smokebox top. Indeed, at first the writer thought it was a tank, for Mitchell experimented unsuccessfully with oil-firing in the early twenties, either on *Sans Pareil* or on *Ella*. He apparently had connections with the Great Eastern and was trying out a modification of Holden's system.

SIR AUBREY TAKES OVER

By 1924, Sir Aubrey's financial stake in the railway was considerable and his natural anxieties must have been increased by his additional investment in Beckfoot. The critical moment appears to have come when, in May 1924, one of the surviving creditors in the old Eskdale Railway Company died and his executors discovered what had been going on. Dawson himself had died in 1917, but his executors were promptly sued for moneys owing to the dead creditor and others joined in.

This was obviously too much for Sir Aubrey to stand as his complete investment was in jeopardy. He decided to take a direct interest in the railway, became a director, and initiated legal proceedings to clear up the whole muddle. Various Actions and Counter-actions were proposed and, eventually, an agreement was reached whereby in consideration of the payment of outstanding debts to the aggrieved parties, Narrow Gauge Railways Limited acquired the freehold of the line and the assets and liabilities of the old Eskdale Company.

Sir Aubrey undoubtedly paid the necessary money to redeem the railway and promptly safeguarded his investment by taking over NGR Limited in partnership with another shipowner, Henry Lithgow. They did this simply by taking up the 998 unpaid-up shares of the original capital, 499 each. Presumably Bassett-Lowke and Mitchell had little or no choice in the matter and, although they were named as 'founder directors' of the re-organised company, they very soon faded from the scene. Mitchell resigned as general manager in February 1925 and left Ravenglass, while Bassett-Lowke had plenty of other affairs to occupy him. Sir Aubrey moved the registered offices to his Cunard Building in Liverpool and put his own nominees in control of operations.

CHAPTER 6

Between the Wars

UNDER NEW MANAGEMENT

The new régime which took over at the beginning of 1925 found the R & E in what amounted to a state of chaos. On every side was evidence that it had been run by model engineers who did not always understand the problems of running a continual service over a long and heavily-graded route. Odd items of Heywood stock such as the sleeping car and bogie ballast wagon had been dumped in the yards, their potential for passenger-carrying neglected, while granite wagons had to be used at peak periods; bits of ironmongery from the radial gear of *Ella* and *Muriel* littered the ground near Murthwaite—it had been disconnected as impracticable but never fully dismantled—and Murthwaite itself was not standing up to the work for which it had been designed.

The old régime had comprised amateur railwaymen; the new masters, if not inspired, were at least professionals who could make the original idea work. William Gillon from Liverpool was a competent general manager and fairly ably supported by the best of the old Mitchell 'finds' and by his new motive power staff—Tom Jones as assistant engineer and Edward 'Ted' Wright as engineer-in-charge. Wright had ideas; some were good, some bad, some merely eccentric, but at least he was ready to take unorthodox measures to deal with the rapidly-worsening motive power situation.

The next five years were full of change: it will be best to deal separately with the changes for clarity, and we will begin with the quarries which were to become the lifeblood of the railway.

THE GRANITE TRAFFIC

Sir Aubrey had begun Beckfoot Granite Quarries Limited as a

separate entity to provide traffic for the railway; local sett-makers had banded together to work the quarry, and Henry Greenly had designed a very neat little crushing plant at Murthwaite to process the stone. It was by all accounts, a beautiful piece of engineering—but built to *model* engineering tolerances and dimensions and hence not very suited to the increasingly heavy load it had to bear. In particular, the elaborate grading device feeding no less than seven grades of crushed stone to hoppers above a fan of 15 in gauge sidings was far too finicky for its job, and the relatively delicate machinery suffered much from the abrasive granite dust with which the crushers filled the air. When Sir Aubrey purchased the railway, the two concerns worked very closely together, at first coming under common management and later, about 1930, being amalgamated. The first thing the new management decided was that Murthwaite would have to be rebuilt. Operations began in 1927, the main line being moved bodily outward from the hill, all the old buildings being cleared, and a new and more robust Symons crusher being installed, fed by a newly-laid siding from the eastern end. A single Campbell oil engine replaced the original Tangye engine which was moved to Beckfoot on 15 February 1929 to drive the compressor there, and the single Campbell was replaced the same August by a twin 210 hp Campbell that lasted until the plant was converted to electricity in 1936. The size of the new crusher and engine-house, work on which was completed in August, meant that the grading screens had to be turned at right angles to their former positions, being served by one long siding instead of the fan of sidings formerly used. (See p 193.)

This rearrangement was in any case desirable as the old sidings had been reached via a sector table at their western end which greatly restricted the size of wagon that could be used, and the new régime wanted to do away with the wagons and the cumbersome tippler at Ravenglass, at least for ballast traffic. Accordingly, six special bogie, bottom-discharge hopper wagons were ordered in July 1927 from the Yorkshire Engine Company, having their first trial some ten months later, on 9 May 1928. The wagons were very successful, greatly streamlining the transhipping arrangements, but their career was extremely short, for plans were already afoot to remove the transhipment problem entirely.

These plans involved the construction of a 2½ mile standard gauge branch starting at an end-on connection with the LMS at Ravenglass on the site of the former tippler and ending under the new screens at Murthwaite. It was impracticable to use a completely new formation, so the branch was laid on the old 3 ft gauge trackbed and the 15 in gauge line was 'gauntletted' between the standard gauge rails from the west end of Murthwaite yard to a point a few hundred yards north of the locomotive shed at Ravenglass. Where the standard and 15 in gauge lines diverged there were fairly complicated and very massive pieces of trackwork known as the Big Points, which were provided with crude but effective interlinked signals and incorporated a heavy swivelling plate to stop 15 in gauge stock dropping into the standard gauge flangeways.

The construction of the branch was carried out with one of the surprising bursts of efficiency which occasionally enlivened the rather bumbling mediocrity of the company's operations. Work began on 4 March 1929 with about twenty men; the line was linked through to Murthwaite by the beginning of July, and the new transfer siding and bridge over the road at Ravenglass were completed on 21 November. This was a very praiseworthy feat, considering that the work involved making up the formation to standard gauge width; lifting all narrow gauge track and replacing the rails on standard-gauge sleepers; slewing the alignment to the north between Katie Caddie and Murthwaite so that it could be lowered (another difficult section, through Mill Wood, had been re-aligned in May 1926); demolishing most of the old embankment at Ravenglass and building a bridge to allow direct connection to the LMS; laying the standard gauge rails in; and connecting up the pointwork.

All this appears to have been done without interrupting the 15 in gauge traffic even in the summer passenger season. The 15 in gauge was re-laid on the standard gauge sleepers as formation and sleeper-laying progressed, and all sleepers were in by 10 May (before the Whitsun opening), while standard gauge track-laying did not begin until the following week.

The completion of the standard gauge led to the cessation of all 15 in gauge stone ballast traffic to Ravenglass LMS, but a good deal of the smaller grades of crushed stone was still run down the narrow gauge from time to time for tipping into road lorries down a chute just behind the engine shed. The railway even kept its own lorry for local deliveries.

The standard gauge motive power, a six-coupled Kerr Stuart diesel locomotive with roller chain drive from a 90 hp MacLaren Benz motor, arrived on 5 December and was tested the following day. It entered regular service at the beginning of 1930, thus affording respite to the hard-pressed 15 in gauge motive power and rendering redundant the superb bogie wagons bought only two years before. These were not needed for roadstone and were sold almost immediately to the R H & D as ballast wagons. One presumes that, during the interim period between completion of the standard gauge and the arrival of the Kerr Stuart, standard gauge wagons were chain—or rope-hauled by narrow gauge tractors; this certainly was the practice in later years when the Kerr Stuart was out of commission.

It is obvious from correspondence that Sir Aubrey and, after he died in 1929, his son, Sir Thomas Brocklebank, were at this period very interested in developing stone traffic to the greatest extent possible for, early in 1930, Ted Wright was asked to submit a detailed report on what more could be done. He estimated that, using existing plant and manpower, an average of about 36,100 tons a year could be extracted from Beckfoot and some 38,000 tons handled at Murthwaite. He suggested that, with practicable improvements—limited by the amount of power available from the twin-Campbell, Murthwaite could handle up to 57,000 tons a year which would not much exceed the capacity of the standard gauge. He therefore prepared estimates:

- i For extending Beckfoot Quarry, at a cost of £3,610
- ii For alternative proposals for quarries west and east of Murthwaite Plant, costing £1,560 or £1,090 respectively

The Beckfoot proposals were expensive because additional motive power and wagons would be required to convey the stone to Murthwaite, while the Murthwaite sites could be served by the plant shunter, and because increasing the quarry capacity would mean extending the face for a hundred yards westward with a danger of running into a fault in the stone and thus not being able to obtain sufficient stone of good quality.

The proposals for Murthwaite had the disadvantage that some months must elapse before a working face was exposed as already-exposed stone would naturally be in a weathered and perished condition and, according to Wright's calculations, it would be five years or more before the quarry was likely to be an economic proposition. The west site, he said, could be brought into production quicker, but the stone was not of very good quality and an embankment and bridge would be needed to carry the high-level siding to the crushing plant over the standard gauge loading sidings. The east site would take longer to develop as a working face, but could be connected directly to the existing feeder siding and the stone was of reasonable quality.

In fact, all his estimates were hypothetical, for stone production from all sources appears never to have exceeded about 20,000 tons a year. Nevertheless, it was decided to open up Murthwaite East Site, and the first blast was fired on 1 June 1932. The quarries were then worked more or less alternately, breaking and clearing of stone going on at one while boring and blasting took place at the other. This made for a fairly leisurely procedure without increasing tonnage very much but did give fairly steady employment to the working force.

Meanwhile, in 1931, the company's main fitting shop, which was established in Ravenglass locomotive shed, was transferred to a new corrugated iron erection alongside the engine house at Murthwaite, perhaps a more logical place for it to be. The transfer was carried out piecemeal during the summer, the shop being formally opened on 30 September 1931.

These activities marked the end of the period of expansion and their full potential was never realised. The depression of 1930-31 probably helped to reduce sales, but there were other influences at work. In particular, the large firms in the stone business, could sell at a price which, while agreed by all concerned, could produce a far larger profit margin than the R & E with its expensive transport costs could hope to achieve, and the remote-control management from Liverpool seems to have exercised little detailed control over operations. In consequence, the company was virtually restricted to local orders and its ballast traffic; the railways always taking a good proportion of Beckfoot stone. This ensured economical use of what stone was won, as ballast took the large grades and the small stone and dust was in demand for roadmaking, but it encouraged the company only to produce sufficient stone overall to meet ballast orders and then to sell the residue. As a result, the stone traffic merely bumbled along from year to year, the company not really trying to expand its activities much beyond assured orders.

LOCOMOTIVES

The quarries represented only one aspect of railway life on the R & E. The line had been re-laid originally with passenger traffic in mind, and the new management realised that a great increase in this would be needed. In consequence great improvements were made to track and buildings and, even more important, to stock, during the first few years of Gillon's management.

At the beginning of 1925, the locomotive department was perhaps the shakiest thing on the railway after Ravenglass station building. The original scale models had taken a terrible hammering; *Sans Pareil* was reduced to light specials and driver-training and, although the other two still took the brunt of seasonal working, age was beginning to tell in odd incidents. *Colossus* shed a driving wheel running into Irton Road on one occasion, and *Sir Aubrey* was soon to fracture her main frame. The traffic was just getting too much for them and they often ran double-headed to handle heavy trains.

In consequence, there was a shortage of motive power and by the 1925 season, *River Esk*, originally designed to haul the heavy stone traffic had been taken off it almost entirely to help with the passengers, leaving stone traffic to the ageing Heywood sisters. *Muriel* struggled gamely with the Beckfoot-Murthwaite trains and *Ella*, in comparatively better condition, handled the Murthwaite-Ravenglass work. The strain on these two was increased by the fact that at peak periods they had to turn out on relief passenger trains; and in *Ella*'s case by a rather shady operation which her boiler had undergone in 1922 or 1923. Shortage of water had caused the crown of her cylindrical firebox to bulge inwards, jamming its brick arch up against her tubeplate. The subsequent repair, apparently carried out by forcibly jacking the bulge back up into something like its original shape, can hardly have been calculated to improve the quality of the boiler! It is not surprising that, by the end of 1926, *Muriel* had been relegated to a steaming boiler at the quarry and *Ella* was needing a complete re-build.

Nor, given Ted Wright's ingenuity, is it surprising that the decision should have been taken to do something drastic with both engines. *Ella* came first, being converted into a petrol locomotive instead of having a new boiler. The new régime had experienced—the correct word one imagines—internal combustion power in the shape of the old Crewe Tractor, which was one of the 'assets' it took over. This, later retrospectively termed ICL No 1, had come to a violent end near Dalegarth one autumn day in 1925 when its flywheel came loose, wrecking the Model 'T' engine. Its spirit, and most of its epicyclic gearbox, had been embodied only a few weeks later in a rather peculiar bogie machine labelled ICL No 1. At the period we are discussing this, which ran through several metamorphoses in its long life and still exists as a tool van, was fitted with a vertically-planked body vaguely resembling an early London underground electric locomotive. It was doing some work but was not very powerful and did not endear itself to drivers as it had at all times to be push-started.

'*Ella* Mk 2' was different. She seems to have exercised a fascination for amateur conversion enthusiasts as plans had already been drawn up for converting her to petrol-electric drive, and the 1927 conversion was equally unusual. It consisted basically of extending the original frames to take a pony truck front and rear, and mounting thereon a sawn-off Lanchester touring car chassis complete with engine and gearbox. Drive was via a Parsons marine reverse gear to elements from the original Lanchester transmission bolted firmly into the frame and thence to the rear drivers, all driving wheels being coupled by the original rods. Unfortunately, the particular Lanchester model was already obsolescent and spare parts were hard to obtain, but she could pull a full stone train and thus afforded great relief to the motive power department. In addition, during the season she regularly pulled the covered Heywood coaches which became thought of as her rake.

In the autumn of 1928 she collided head-on with the Ford ICL No 1, reducing the latter's body to matchwood and distorting her own none-too strong frame. Although the frame was more or less straightened she was never quite the same afterwards and, after a gruelling time during the icy winter that followed, she ran a big-end through her crank-case in the spring of 1929. It was almost impossible to obtain spare parts and, having regard to the damage already caused, she was withdrawn and scrapped by instalments. The frames were still lying at Murthwaite when the present company took over thirty years later! She was later replaced by three Muir-Hill Fordson-powered tractors which arrived in 1928-9, one being rebuilt as an 0–4–4D after her demise to handle passenger traffic.

Meanwhile, back at the shops... The other steam locomotives were also nearing the end of their lives. *Sans Pareil* had to be withdrawn at the end of the 1926 season; it was obvious that, by the end of the following season, *Colossus* and *Sir Aubrey* would be finished; and, to crown all, *Esk* was running erratically, her Lentz poppet valve gear never being really satisfactory.

With characteristic ingenuity the motive power department decided to tackle the arrears of work all at once, largely on a 'do-it-yourself' basis. *River Esk* was sent away to the Yorkshire Engine Company for a professional re-build into an articulated locomotive

Page 75: VIGNETTES OF THE 20S

[*above*] *Relief working in the Mitchell era. 'Ella' pauses for breath at Irton Road with a crowded third or fourth portion.* [*below*] *Pomp and pride of the new regime. Ravenglass rebuilt, with the three 'home-built' locomotives and the rebuilt 'Esk', all lined up for Mary Fair*

Page 76: INTRODUCTION TO INTERNAL COMBUSTION

[above] Wall Autowheel scooter (which collided with 'Sans Pareil') seen here on 'mail run' at Beckfoot. Only known photograph showing top end of Beckfoot loop. [below] Crewe Tractor, alias Model 'T' Ford, successor to the Autowheel, being turned on its built-in turning plate at Irton Road. Note Heywood sleeping car acting as store in background

on the Poultney system, acquiring Walschaerts valve gear in the process, but *Muriel* and the two scale models were rebuilt at Ravenglass with Yorkshire Engine Company boilers, a fairly considerable feat with the resources available.

Muriel was tackled first. The old Heywood frames and running gear were still serviceable and it was decided simply to fit a conventional locomotive boiler and 'scale-model' cab, extending the main frames rearward over a pair of idler wheels to carry the firebox. The conversion was straightforward, the trials caused no major headaches, and the locomotive went into service on 1 August, being renamed *River Irt* and proving very successful.

This conversion encouraged Wright and company to an even more ambitious operation, nothing less than the amalgamation of *Colossus* and *Sir Aubrey* into a single articulated locomotive. Following the end of the 1927 season, both locomotives were stripped down completely, their boilers scrapped, and the best wheels from all three scale models assembled into the frames. These in turn were mounted under each end of a massive frame unit carrying boiler, cab, and tender body. Work was held up by protracted trials of the rebuilt *River Esk* during January 1928 but, after the boiler arrived on 25 February, completion was rapid and the new locomotive was tried under steam at the end of March. There were naturally teething troubles, but all were sorted out by the opening of the passenger season and the railway was then in a far more satisfactory motive power position than it had been a year before.

TRACK AND BUILDINGS

Quarry and locomotives were not the only items to need extension and improvement. With the upsurge of passenger traffic during the 1926 season it became obvious that improvements were also needed in passenger handling facilities.

First priority was the moving of Dalegarth terminus to a more convenient and accessible spot than its pleasant but inconspicuous site below Dalegarth Cottages. During August 1926, therefore, the line was extended over the Whillan beck on a much-reinforced version of the old tramway bridge and extended along the route of the Gill Force branch as far as the main road up Eskdale, the necessary land being purchased for £190. Permission could not be obtained for a level crossing and the terminus was built on the site of the old loading stages on a narrow piece of made-up ground.

The difficulties of the ground plan were overcome by ending the line in a turntable and by building the station out to the west partly on piles where the ground sloped sharply away. It was intended from the beginning to continue the practice of serving refreshments at the upper terminus, always a profitable source of revenue as the railway terminated some distance from such comforts. Accordingly, during November 1927, a large wooden hut from the Home Office Establishment at Eskmeals was acquired and erected forming the present café.

Initially, just a single siding was provided but, in December 1926, this was changed to a three-track layout with turntable to enable two trains to be stabled at once and still leave free an engine escape road. This existed for some years, but the narrow site rendered it somewhat dangerous, Heywood coaches in particular tending to foul the platform when their doors were open—a problem which soon led to the removal of most of the doors because of incidental damage. During the winter of 1932-3, the layout was changed to the present two-track one with a long stock siding stretching back towards Beckfoot from the down end of the run-round loop.

Little was done to intermediate stations, although the rickety wooden huts at halts disappeared piecemeal, while Irton Road was plastered with posters on the stone hut and there were heaps of rotting junk in the station yard. Something *had* to be done at Ravenglass, where the old 3 ft gauge train shed was rotting away and hampering operations when two or more trains were loading at the same time. During the winter of 1927-8 the layout was cleared and completely rebuilt—a purgative habit of the 15 in gauge line which appears to recur approximately every twenty years!

The new layout (see pp 191-2) retained the original end turntable with its fan of short stock sidings but had four main tracks with three platform faces, a neat island platform in stone-edged gravel serving the two centre roads. A modest waiting shelter graced the site of the old train shed and a ticket office was sited near the entrance to the LMS yard. The whole thing was a decided improvement on what had gone before and blended in nicely with the wooden buildings which had been erected by the Mitchell régime in the early 1920s. These were a bungalow; a wooden carriage shed on the east side of the line, and a ramshackle wooden extension to the old locomotive shed. The locomotive shed extension was blown flat about 1928 but the other two still survive, although the carriage shed has recently been partly rebuilt.

An ephemeral construction was erected when the 'broad gauge' was put in. This was a simple wooden shelter over the interchange siding, some fifty yards north of the road bridge at Ravenglass. Consisting only of a pitched roof supported on wooden posts, it can have given the Kerr Stuart little protection from the rain-laden winds off the estuary and succumbed after the war when large hopper wagons were introduced and needed larger clearances.

ROLLING-STOCK

Improvements in other spheres were not at once matched elsewhere. True, all available Heywood-type closed vehicles were either patched up or completely rebuilt very soon after the new régime took over, but their age precluded any great lengthening of their lives. By 1931, Gillon was noting that four of the seven were unserviceable with rotten woodwork (they had wood framing) and they last ran in regular passenger service about 1934. No further closed vehicles were built to replace them.

The open Heywoods, too, were ageing rapidly and a start was made in 1928 on replacements. Six were built at Ravenglass during the 1928 season. These were very similar in concept except that a flush floor was fitted, thus enabling the Heywood pattern of end balcony to be replaced by extra seats. They formed the pattern for twelve more constructed during the 1930s mainly to replace the closed stock and the Bassett-Lowke four-wheelers, which were also falling to pieces.

GENERAL NOTES

The late 1920s, then, saw a tremendous burst of activity on the railway, mainly because of the energetic if slightly eccentric ingenuity of Ted Wright as engineer and also because of the enthusiasm and support of Sir Aubrey, whose money provided the capital needed for reconstruction. In retrospect, it seems amazing how much was done so well and so quickly for, with outside labour as required, the company staff not only renewed motive power and rolling-stock but also completely reconstructed Murthwaite Plant—which after all was the equivalent of a small factory—and in effect built a new 2½ mile-long standard gauge railway. This, it must be remembered, was in the post-war depression period, with strikes and falling prices to hamper efforts.

Sir Aubrey's interest was purely personal and, when he died in April 1929, the railway suffered an irreparable loss. His successor, Sir Thomas Brocklebank, and his old partner, Henry Lithgow, saw the reconstruction through, but otherwise took little interest in the line. They were busy men, without Sir Aubrey's personal involvement, and neither the railway nor the quarry was ever likely to make enough profit to be financially worthwhile to them. Indeed it is to their credit that, in Sir Aubrey's memory, the railway was allowed to continue instead of being put up for sale.

Yet there might have been advantages for the railway in a sale to someone directly interested in the line for its own sake. Such a sale had actually been in prospect early in 1925 when Captain Howey was looking for somewhere to build a railway. He offered to buy the R & E, proposing to extend it to Ambleside, but Sir Aubrey refused to sell. It may have been this contact that led to trials of *Green Goddess*, the first RH & D 'Pacific', being held on the R & E later the same year.

Certainly for the R & E, remote control from a largely-uninterested Liverpool office, the main requirement of which was that as little money as possible should be spent, did not make for aggressive or efficient local management, especially as there appears to have been some coolness between Gillon and Wright during the 1930s. Ted Wright suffered a bad leg injury in 1934 and was never the same afterwards, and the R & E settled down to a comfortable mediocre existence. There was little or no attempt to expand the quarrying and stone-selling operations, the amount of small stone always depending on the size of LMS ballast orders, and little more was done to locomotives and stock after the construction of the passenger tractor. The winter service had gone with the postal contract in 1927-8, only a Thursday market service being retained, and even that finished in 1937. In fact, the line went into a slow but steady decline so that what had in 1930 been a well-found, attractive, and efficient railway had, by the outbreak of the second world war, acquired a somewhat seedy air. *River Esk* was in very poor condition, *River Mite* had proved to have considerable design defects and had been lying partly dismantled at Ravenglass since 1937, and most of the work was being borne by *River Irt* and the Fordson 0–4–4.

CHAPTER 7

The Second World War and After

THE WAR

When the second world war broke out on 3 September 1939 the railway was nearing the end of another uneventful season. Passenger traffic was discontinued at the end of September as usual and did not begin again for another six years. Tourists had no place in wartime Britain and materials were scarce, so the two steam locomotives were put in store, *River Esk* being partly dismantled for a much-needed overhaul.

The quarrying side of the company's activities and the resultant railway traffic still continued working although under increasing difficulties as materials and labour became scarce. Fortunately the Kerr Stuart was able to have a major overhaul late in 1941 and all three Fordson tractors were then in good condition.

Problems naturally arose, and Tom Jones' annual reports from Murthwaite tell their own story. In 1942 all was reasonably secure on the railway, with one tractor working in and around the quarry, and two shuttling back and forth between the quarry and Murthwaite. The main stock problem was the wagons, the iron doors of which were very worn and required replacement. In the crushing plant itself, the Symons machine required constant attention and certain of the wooden buildings were showing signs of decay, but it was planned to replace them with concrete. All work was done at Murthwaite, worn parts on both Kerr Stuart and Symons being replaced or built up by railway staff.

1943 was much the same in the motive power department, all the Fordsons getting complete overhauls. The quarry one which did not come into contact with the very abrasive dust thrown out by the crushing plant had achieved the respectable period of two and a half years between overhauls. The wagons were giving constant trouble, the worn wheels showing a tendency to break and de-rail vehicles: this naturally caused further damage which could be ill-afforded. The track too was causing anxiety:

> Every sleeper between Murthwaite and Ravenglass is rotten, and whenever derailments occur, no sleepers are available to replace broken ones.

records the report for that year. Accordingly experiments were carried out with concrete sleepers cast at Murthwaite; these were quite successful but, once again, shortage of materials limited the number that could be made.

1944 showed further deterioration all round. The Kerr Stuart's gearbox had to be patched up at Leeds, as no spare parts were available, and all tractor engines were badly worn, while most wagon doors had worn so thin as not to be repairable. The track was still deteriorating, although over sixty concrete sleepers had been laid on the broad gauge section. The crushing plant on the other hand gave surprisingly little trouble throughout the year, and the supplementary wooden bins were replaced by concrete ones.

1945 saw the end of the war, but there was little chance of obtaining materials for proper repairs and a policy of make-do and mend had to continue, with a plant now showing the signs of cumulative neglect. In particular, the Symons machine was getting very worn, its foundations causing some anxiety through subsidence, and the quarry compressors had lost enough efficiency to cause serious problems in drilling. On the credit side, the tractor engines had been replaced by reconditioned units.

Conditions eased a little and, in 1946, the railway was able to start the climb—or rather scramble—back to a reasonable state of efficiency. A new compressor was bought for Beckfoot, plates became available for fabricating wagon doors, and a limited passenger service was reinstated during the summer albeit with only the passenger tractor as power. It also proved possible to give some attention to *River Irt*, which was re-tubed, re-tyred, and fitted with new pistons in readiness for the 1947 season. Unfortunately *Esk* needed a full overhaul and *Mite* had been partly dismantled. Its 'power bogies' had been sold to Barlow of Southport as they were of little further use and, although Wright had had ideas for rebuilding it, on his departure in 1943 no one else felt that the job would be really worthwhile. The bits lingered on in the back of the shed together with the old Poultney unit from *River Esk*.

Wright was not the only Brocklebank nominee to leave. William Gillon resigned at the beginning of 1946 and Harry Hilton was appointed to the thankless task of restoring a very run-down system with little financial backing. Some effort was made, but the directorate was not nearly as interested in the railway as it had been in Sir Aubrey's day. Indeed, but for Henry Lithgow the Brocklebank family might well have disposed of the company earlier. Lithgow was ailing now and, when he died on 24 November 1948, there was no longer any obstacle to the sale of NGR assets.

THE KESWICK GRANITE COMPANY

A buyer was soon found. Although sales had been erratic, Beckfoot granite in particular was of very fine quality and its production had been a constant irritation to the big Keswick Granite Company of Threlkeld. This company seized the opportunity to acquire a potentially dangerous competitor, achieving its end on 1 July 1949 by purchasing the £1,000 nominal share capital of NGR Limited, together with all its assets and liabilities, for a valuation of £12,888 0s 9d. The company thus retained its name but became a wholly-owned subsidiary of the Keswick concern.

The change of ownership brought no immediate changes to the railway. The management was still left to go its own way, and no positive attempt was made to increase the sales of granite or the efficiency of the quarry and crushing plant. It is true that the most notable event in the quarry's history took place after Keswick Granite had assumed control, but it had been planned some while previously. It was heralded by the following notice advertised rather unusually in the local press:

BLASTING
AT ESKDALE QUARRY

The Narrow Gauge Railways, Ravenglass, HEREBY GIVE NOTICE that Blasting Operations will take place in Beckfoot Quarry, Eskdale, Cumberland on Saturday August 20th 1949 at 12.30 p.m. No unauthorised persons will be allowed on the quarry premises that day. A warning signal will be given 10 minutes before firing time.

Signed: H. Hilton
General Manager.

This prosaic warning concealed the biggest firing ever to take place in Eskdale quarrying, designed to bring down in one operation no less than 50,000 tons of granite. Preparatory work under the

Page 85: HEYWOOD DUTIES

[above] Typical duty for an older locomotive. 'Muriel' leaving Irton Road, hauling relief passenger train during peak period. [below] Also 'Muriel', ambling along toward Ravenglass with a train of stone for Murthwaite crusher

Page 86: VARIED WORK

[above] General goods traffic at Irton Road, with a train of granite empties in the background. [below] Unloading 'Green Goddess' at Ravenglass, showing also in the rear glass coach and Heywood dining car and Heywood open on the right. Note (left) pristine condition of allegedly 30-year-old closed coaches

Page 87: PROBLEMS

[above] 'River Eske' on ballasting work during realignment of track in Mill Wood around 1927. [below] Down train chasing another at Irton Road during busy period. Photograph also shows locomotive shed and Heywood bogie wagon upside-down by lineside

Page 88: RENEWAL AT RAVENGLASS

Before and after the new regime. [above] Ravenglass in 1921. [below] Ravenglass rebuilt in 1928. Photograph shows bungalow, carriage shed and, in the background, original locomotive shed with wooden extension, with trans-shipment gantry on left direction of Tom Jones had been going on for nearly six months before, almost 200 tons of granite being excavated from a 50 ft-long tunnel driven into the quarry face, with 30 ft-long transverse tunnels driven from its far end parallel with the face.

The actual firing was quite a festive occasion, the directors of Keswick Granite Company and their invited guests—who included both pressmen and representatives of local amenity societies—journeying up the R & E by special train and taking lunch in the railway's Dalegarth Café. The blast was highly successful—in the words of the local paper:

> From behind the 50 ft of solid granite came a muffled explosion and the whole face of the 150 ft high quarry moved forward. The ground for several hundred yards shook violently as though affected by an earthquake.
> In the quarry itself, granite estimated at 50,000 tons crashed to the ground and a dense column of dust rose into the air. For some considerable time afterwards huge masses of rock were crashing into the quarry.

The Keswick Granite party prudently watched from the far side of the River Esk and was most satisfied. It was estimated that the rock dislodged would provide work for two or three years before any further blasting was required. No serious damage had occurred to the surrounding neighbourhood, and even the rural preservation societies could find little about which to grumble.

The blast was the last major quarrying operation carried out at Beckfoot. By the time its remains had been finally removed early in 1953, conditions on the R & E had deteriorated so much that the Keswick Granite Company decided to ask its assistant manager, Mr Graham, to investigate the whole NGR operation.

Mr Graham confined himself to the stone-quarrying and carrying aspects of NGR Limited and produced an extremely thorough report. He found the position very unsatisfactory in several respects. In particular, there was great difficulty in obtaining sufficient labour at the quarry, mainly because of a housing shortage, and this in turn reflected on the general state of the railway. Murthwaite was in a mess and not very efficient, and the standard gauge line was unsafe for regular working, while all quarrying and crushing equipment was badly worn. He concluded that the annual tonnage, at about 14,000, was in step with sales but needed to be increased to about 21,000 tons to make full use of the facilities available.

He suggested that the most sensible action would be to close down Murthwaite quarry and plant completely for the summer of 1953, when sales dropped off sharply in any case, and to use the time and labour to rejuvenate the plant and to improve the quarry at Beckfoot while building up stocks by limited quarrying operations there. He also advised the construction of an access road from Murthwaite to the main valley road at Sandbank, a move which, if it had materialised, would undoubtedly have taken much traffic from the railway.

The road was never built. On receiving Graham's report the Keswick Granite Company decided that the expense involved in re-building, together with the staffing problem, was too great and that, instead, it would close down all quarrying operations at Beckfoot and dismantle Murthwaite crushing plant. On strict economic terms, it was probably right to do this as the operation had never come near to breaking even, let alone making a profit, but one cannot help feeling that Keswick Granite never had any real interest in maintaining production from Beckfoot once it had bought out NGR Limited thus ending competition. Perhaps the real fault lay even deeper, in the lack of management interest and supervision dating from the time of Sir Aubrey's death. Following closure, the name of Narrow Gauge Railways Limited was changed to the South Cumberland Granite Company, presumably to draw customers, but all orders were fulfilled from Threlkeld or Midgeholme quarries.

None the less, Keswick Granite did not lose interest entirely in the railway and indeed encouraged the development of passenger traffic while completely separating passenger and granite aspects of the work. *River Esk* had been overhauled and returned to traffic in 1952 and, in 1955, on Tom Jones' recommendation, work was even authorised on a new diesel locomotive. This unit, a 4–6–4 designed round some parts of *Ella* and a Fordson diesel engine, was partly completed when, in 1957, the subvention provisions of the 1953 Finance Act were modified so that it was no longer possible for losses of subsidiary companies to be set off against a parent company's profits. Once the concession was withdrawn, the R & E became a very definite liability to its parent and the Granite Company offered the railway for sale, excluding Beckfoot Quarry and its approach road so that no one could set up in competition again! Apart from some unsuccessful negotiations by a wealthy Birmingham stockbroker and miniature railway enthusiast, Mr Colin Gilbert, no offers were received: negotiations with Mr Gilbert broke down because of the vagueness of the title deeds.

UP FOR SALE AGAIN

Advertisements appeared during September 1958 in several newspapers. The following, in the *Daily Telegraph* of 4 September, was typical:

> For sale as a going concern by Private Treaty. Ravenglass and Eskdale Miniature Railway. In the Lake District of Cumberland. 7½ miles of 15 in gauge track up beautiful Eskdale. Two model steam and three diesel locomotives. Well-maintained rolling-stock, station buildings, repair shops and wagon sheds. 11 houses, cafe, shop and land comprising the well fenced and wooded permanent way, 3 fields and various open spaces. Inclusive price, £22,500 Freehold. For further information apply to T. Graham, General Manager, Keswick Granite Co. Ltd.

No purchaser was forthcoming and, apparently unconcerned, the company continued to operate the line for the 1959 season, offering it for sale once more in August of that year at an unspecified price for complete or part sale.

One offer of £4,000 was received for the rails and sleepers only, but by this time it was obvious that the company genuinely wanted to see the line remain as a going concern and was prepared to wait even longer if this could be arranged. Unfortunately, although two virtually competing groups of enthusiasts were making desultory efforts to raise capital, nothing concrete was done and it was not until the line's demise seemed certain that they agreed to sink their differences. A body calling itself the Ravenglass & Eskdale Railway Preservation Society was formed and buckled down to active fund-raising.

The crucial factor was the Keswick company's decision that it would have to offer the track and plant for sale by auction. The auction was announced in July 1960 to take place on 10 August at the neighbouring village of Gosforth, which boasts a good-sized hall. At the last moment it was postponed for a further month to enable the R & E R P S to make a final effort to raise sufficient funds.

The sale, on a mid-week afternoon, 7 September, attracted a considerable crowd, between 300 and 400 people packing the hall. Most were obviously local inhabitants, but scrap dealers were also present in force as were the representatives of the Preservation Society. The society itself had managed to raise only some £5,000, but its efforts were backed by Mr Colin Gilbert, the Midlands stockbroker who had been negotiating with Keswick Granite on his own behalf for some years. Thus, after some tense moments, Mr Douglas Robinson, Clerk of the Muncaster Council, was able to make the winning bid of £12,000 on behalf of the preservation society. The bid was accepted and the line, for the moment at any rate, was saved.

An interesting point about the sale was that, if no acceptable bid for the complete railway had been received, the component parts would have been sold off in sixty different 'lots', but one lot, comprising a short section of line near Murthwaite, would have been retained to ensure that no one was able to put the lots together again and thus make a complete railway. The Granite Company retained the quarries with rights of way to each.

As noted, the R & E R P S had only £5,000 capital, and the balance of the purchase price, totalling some £6,800 was put up by Mr Gilbert, Sir Wavell Wakefield (a local landowner) offering further support if required. In the event, this was not needed, Mr Gilbert being prepared to maintain the railway (staff wages, etc) for the forthcoming winter out of his own pocket. It was therefore natural that, like Sir Aubrey before him, he wished to have control of his investment. An agreement was reached by which an operating company, the Ravenglass & Eskdale Railway Co Ltd, was formed in March 1961, the majority shareholder being Mr Gilbert. The society's £5,000 was accepted as loan capital which could not be redeemed without the society's consent. Operation of the railway was to be by a full-time staff employed by the company, and the society pledged itself to provide financial support and voluntary labour for certain responsibilities the chief of which are year-round maintenance work and the provision of additional guards in the peak season.

YET ANOTHER NEW MANAGEMENT

The new company took over its property almost at once. Mr Douglas Ferreira was appointed general manager, Tom Jones (who had been doing both the manager's and engineer's work since Harry Hilton's retirement in 1959), thankfully returning to his indispensable role of engineer. The remainder of the former employees who wished to remain were retained in the new organisation.

Immediately after take-over, work began on bringing the railway up to a high standard. As with most preservation operations, the state of the track and locomotives was causing much concern and, as a stop-gap measure, both steam locomotives were re-tubed in the winter of 1960-61 while the passenger tractor was re-engined. An extensive track-relaying programme was initiated and the workshops were moved piecemeal from Murthwaite to the engine shed and the old carriage shed at Ravenglass. Finally, following trials in the spring of 1961, an experimental B-B diesel-hydraulic locomotive *Royal Anchor* was purchased. This last has not been wholly successful, the locomotive having several inherent design defects and being unable to haul more than four or five laden bogie coaches, but it does provide a useful power unit for light trains, easing the load on a deteriorating passenger tractor. The six 1923-vintage four-wheelers were converted to semi-opens, by adding ends and roofs, to form a regular train for *Royal Anchor* and, for their first season only, ran as a named train, the *Rambler*.

Urgent work continued through the following winter and during 1962. A full list of improvements would be tedious, but one should mention the contracting-out to Rentokil of a weed-killing contract, initially for the top half of the line only, and the installation of a private GPO telephone line between Ravenglass and Irton Road. Perhaps even more interesting was the revival of the winter passenger service in October 1962. This, a daily working down to Ravenglass in the morning and back to Dalegarth in the evening on Mondays to Fridays only, was primarily for staff transport; in the Mitchell tradition, however, it was scheduled as an advertised train and has continued as such each winter.

1962-3, too, saw the re-building of coaches 13-18 and the provision of a new firebox for *River Irt*. 1963 itself was something of a climacteric. It opened on a sad note with the death of Harry Hilton on 21 February and, from the railway point of view, was extremely busy. Main items of note were the lifting of all usable rail from Beckfoot Quarry in March; the arrival on 4 April of a camping coach to provide accommodation for society volunteers; the commencement of excavations for new carriage sidings at Ravenglass and the official naming of the surviving Muir Hill 0–4–0D as *Quarryman*—notwithstanding which, it has continued to be called 'Billy's Tractor' after its driver, Billy Bell.

Perhaps the most exciting events since the take-over occurred in the autumn. On 19 October, the society formally decided to order a new steam locomotive similar to *River Esk*. Construction was to be by Clarkson of York, making use of the old Poultney tender chassis from *Esk* as a basis. The locomotive, to be named *River Mite*, was to be owned by the society and loaned to the railway. Construction was estimated at three years, dependent on finance, and meanwhile *River Esk*'s boiler was completely rebuilt by Gower of Bedford to give that locomotive a new lease of life.

In the autumn of 1963, it seemed that the railway might once again carry regular goods traffic, for a local firm called Redblock Precast Concrete was formed to exploit the vast quantities of granite dust dumped at Murthwaite and the railway contracted to move the finished blocks to Irton Road. The venture started well with a load of 500 blocks on 9 October and, by early 1964, sufficient traffic had been generated for a special siding to be put in at Irton Road. Alas, the firm did not prosper, and all work has since been discontinued, Irton Road siding being turned over to the PW Department.

At the end of the year the carriage sidings were completed and the first major realignment for nearly forty years made to the track. Mr Gilbert personally paid for a new cutting at Hollinghead to obviate the sharp reverse curves needed to round Hollinghead Bluff. Twelve feet deep at its deepest and 400 ft long, the cutting involved removing some 3,000 tons of stone and earth. It was opened on 27 March 1964 by a formal ceremony and the passage of the 11.20 am ex Ravenglass, the first train of the season. At about the same time a complete set of mileposts was installed on the line.

1964 also saw the closure of Ravenglass BR goods yard and of the R & E's private siding under the Beeching rationalisation plan; the commencement of work in July on *River Mite;* the replacement mid-October of the badly-corroded 15 in gauge bridge at Ravenglass by the girders formerly carrying the standard gauge siding, and the first operating profit since 1894: about £1,000!

END OF AN ERA

1965 was comparatively quiet, although in October the line once again saw closed coaches in the shape of three, eight-seater bogie saloons from New Brighton, together with an 18-inch gauge Ruston & Hornsby diesel locomotive. The locomotive was soon sold on but the coaches were regauged and remained in service until 1978. Otherwise, 1966 saw several signs of progress. . .and the end of the block traffic although its relics lay around Muncaster for a long time afterward. On the track, all but a few of the standard gauge sleepers between Ravenglass and Murthwaite were replaced, a new concrete and asbestos carriage shed with four-roads capacity was erected in December over the new sidings and Ravenglass station suffered another of its periodic convulsions. At the end of the year, the station was completely stripped and, during early 1967, was relaid as shown in the Atlas, two main platforms and a bay being built while a scissors crossover replaced the former complex of points at the station throat. The components of 'Tom Jones' diesel were sent away for incorporation into a new machine but this turned out to be the last fling of the old regime. In 1968, Colin Gilbert died and the railway's future was once more under review.

The death of Mr Gilbert can be said to have marked the end of the first period of the preservation era. In eight years since takeover, the 'new' company had caught up on a considerable backlog of maintenance and had, in many departments, been able to make noticeable improvements; but progress had been the steady climb-back expected of a preserved railway rather than anything spectacular. The preservation society was, in general, happy with the way things were going and was hopeful that it would now be able to take control of what many members still regarded as 'their' railway. . .but this was not to be.

CHAPTER 8

A More Commercial Concern

The Society's hopes were quickly dashed when it was learnt that control had actually passed to Colin Gilbert's associate Lord Wakefield of Kendal (as Sir Wavell Wakefield had by now become). There was, initially, much disappointment and, indeed, a degree of apprehension since the new owner was thought of as someone remote and likely to have very little real interest in the railway. Fortunately for the railway, this was not true although considerable changes were certainly on the way. While Colin Gilbert and the preservationists were railway enthusiasts in the traditional mould, Lord Wakefield was much more concerned with the Lake District and its prosperity in general. Thus it is probably fair to say that he regarded the railway much as Sir Aubrey Brocklebank had done—as a desirable attraction and provider of employment but one which would, so far as possible, have to pay its own way. It would thus be susceptible to pressures for modernisation and diversification of activities which might not be regarded with total favour by dedicated preservationists. It is probably a tribute to his obvious sincerity and goodwill that the Society proved able to accept the situation and work with the new regime; it was undoubtedly helped by the fact that at local level the management and staff remained largely unchanged. It is one of the company's strengths that it has continuity of staff and is very much a family in itself; as with most families there is a fair amount of grumbling at times but it is noticeable that very few indeed give up and go away.

Indeed, to an outside historian, the fifteen years from 1968 to Lord Wakefield's death have decided parallels with the years of the Brocklebank regime, even if forestry and outside consultancy substituted for granite quarrying. . .and, as with that similar period of activity in the 1920s and 1930s, it seems sensible to divide it up into 'areas' rather than just to produce a chronological list of events especially since most of the major post-war initiatives matured during this period. Let us look first, then, at the physical developments which

Page 97: BOTH ENDS OF THE LINE

[above] *Ravenglass Station from main line: a vintage shot.* [below] *'River Irt', as first rebuilt, stands ready to depart from Dalegarth on the three-track layout. Note the short platform*

Page 98: REBUILT POWER

[*above*] *Rebuilt 'Esk', with Poultney articulated tender engine.* [*centre*] 0–8–2 *tender locomotive 'River Irt', formerly 'Muriel'.* [*below*] *Gallant but unsuccessful attempt: the first 'River Mite' (from 'Sir Aubrey Brocklebank' and 'Colossus')*

Lord Wakefield encouraged and secondly at some highlights of the historical scene. The developments were major and illustrated the positive side of belonging to a large and commercially minded organisation; if the railway was to become more viable it was accepted that capital investment was necessary and, because of the breadth of Lord Wakefield's interests, the resources were available, at least during the 1970s.

OPERATIONAL CHANGES

Probably the most significant set of changes was in the methods of actually operating the railway. At the beginning of the period, operating methods were very traditional—almost hallowed by tradition, one might say and harking back to the Mitchell era. Train services were run effectively by timetable and telephone with comparatively few scheduled trains but running often in two or occasionally in three portions on a time-delay system and crossing en-masse at Irton Road, though Murthwaite was also used. With the vast increase in leisure and in car ownership during the late 1960s and early 1970s, a schedule effectively geared to the comings and goings of BR was increasingly inflexible. A plan was, therefore, drawn up to provide two further passing loops, splitting the line into four sections and operating by centralised train control from Ravenglass signalbox using radio telephones as a reporting mechanism. This was installed using telephones initially (they would be needed eventually as a fall-back system anyway). Meanwhile a German friend of the railway had come up with a scheme for working by radio on the continental model. With his help, a usable system was designed and installed, suitable operational procedures being 'rattyfied' from a rule book used by the Austrian Zillertalbahn—which in turn had adapted it from that used by a north German railway. The result (see p. 167 for details) may not be quite what either of its progenitors envisaged but appears eminently sensible and adapted to its purpose. Its initial trials were marred by an unfortunate collision during the interim period of working on telephone, *Shelagh of Eskdale* and *River Esk* meeting head-on in section. Fortunately no one was killed or seriously injured and it did emphasise the fact that strict rules of procedure were needed even for modern control systems. It also, perhaps, was timely in drawing attention to a design weakness in some of the older coaches which were promptly withdrawn. (It also, incidentally, showed the superior strength of modern motive power; *Shelagh*, with her rigid frame, was barely dented while poor *Esk's* front end was sadly bent.) Once the radio link was fully established, however, the system proved both safe and flexible and the R & E R can justly be said to have pioneered the use of radio-link control in this country. It is simple and robust and not the same as the elaborate computer-generated 'electronic token' methods now being adopted by BR; indeed it may well be considered superior in that it actively encourages responsibility and vigilance among the train crews.

The combined flexibility of the new system and the extra loops has also revolutionised actual operation in that trains can, if need be, operate at 20 minute intervals and the need for relief portions has disappeared; there are sufficient paths for the controller to insert extra timetabled trains on busy days. It may be noted in this context that the additional loops are not passenger stations. The line is now a highly efficient people carrier, set up to move the largest number likely to descend on it at peak periods while being able to cope easily with fluctuations.

Operations have changed in another way also. The railway has always claimed that it provides year-round services, mainly on the basis of running a morning train down and an evening train back. Even though mainly for the benefit of staff, these do take any public traffic offering and the railway as a tourist attraction no longer shuts down from mid-September until the following spring. Weekend services extend throughout the year, while the Christmas period, complete with Santa Specials and other activities, is becoming quite busy.

So far as the 'peripherals' are concerned, there have also been changes, though evolutionary rather than revolutionary ones. For example, tickets no longer tend to come off a roll, Edmundson card tickets being the norm, while family and runabout tickets at reduced rates encourage groups who might otherwise be put off by the inevitably rising fares. Increased concern with safety has meant that the hand brakes characteristic of the 1960s era now simply supplement automatic airbrakes with all vehicles piped and an ever-increasing proportion actually brake-fitted.

LOCOMOTIVES AND STOCK

Part of the capital investment ensured a steady, if slow, improvement in the locomotive and rolling stock fleet. So far as motive power was concerned, the first significant move was a decision to build a new steam locomotive at Ravenglass, utilising a standard R & E R boiler and employing existing formers. There was considerable discussion as to what this locomotive should be like, designs (back of the envelope variety) ranging from Lough Swilly-type 4–6–2s to colonial outline machines. All had in common a six-coupled chassis and the idea that they should be narrow gauge rather than miniature in outline—the railway was at this time suffering a reaction against scale models partly because of their visual incongruity with the maximum loading gauge stock. Following lessons learnt from Northern Chief's visit in 1971 the eventual design was a handsome and well proportioned 2–6–2 tender engine with laminated leaf springing. It was named, prosaically, *Northern Rock* after the Building Society which sponsored it, thus breaking the tradition of River names (but then the next logical River name would have been Whillan Beck which does not sound particularly euphonious either!). It came into service in 1976 and has since been regarded both as the railway's flagship and as a prototype for others which the company offers to build for outside customers.

Northern Rock was conceived from the start as a narrow gauge machine and looks the part. The same cannot entirely be said of *River Irt*, rebuilt to a narrow gauge outline in 1971-2, since the combination of Heywood chassis, a low-set standard boiler (fitted 1978) and a 'grafted-on' cab and boiler fittings is not quite so successful visually—though a vast improvement on what it was like before. The rebuild does, however, reflect an intention to maintain and improve the existing stud, demonstrated also in a 1983 reboilering of *River Esk*. Largely stemming from Lord Wakefield's interest in the application of modern technology to traditional equipment, *Esk* was modified to have a gas-combustion firebox on L. D. Porta's principles. The use of these techniques on such a small machine was greeted with some scepticism, but it has proved surprisingly successful. Certainly the locomotive steams—and steams well—on small coal of a quality the others would reject, though whether the experiment, with all its complications is worth repeating, has not been decided. Nonetheless it won the premier Coal Board award for technological innovation in 1986.

The other existing steam locomotive, *River Mite*, continued at work as a useful member of the stud during this period but the railway still felt the need for additional steam power. In true Ratty tradition, Ravenglass shops therefore turned their attention to an elderly 2 ft gauge 0–4–0WT from Dundee Gasworks which a friend of the railway, Ian Fraser, had offered if it was of any use. The boiler and chassis were basically sound and the Works decided to take it in hand as the basis of a light tank engine. The result emerged in May 1982 as a narrow gauge 0–4–2T with side tanks and a full cab with detachable rear portion. After a few teething troubles, she proved capable of hauling a six coach train and has become a useful member of the stud.

The diesel stud also saw considerable revision during the period. Existing members were rebuilt from time to time to increase their efficiency, *Shelagh* receiving a new Perkins engine in 1979 with a better hydraulic transmission and being repainted in two-tone green. She has since spent considerable periods away from the railway, first 'proving' diesel traction on the Romney line and then working at the 1984 Liverpool Garden Festival. The Passenger Tractor first obtained a similar engine in 1975 and then, virtually worn out mechanically, was taken into shops and rebuilt in 1984 to a modern diesel shunter. As regards new machines, the railway had for some time felt a need for a light unit capable of running early and late trains and of undertaking what were then envisaged as shuttle services to and from Muncaster Mill. A newly delivered saloon coach (No 126) was therefore modified in 1976 to incorporate a Ford power unit driving one bogie through hydraulic transmission and, still in its coach livery, actually took part in the centenary cavalcade of the year. During the winter it was properly rebuilt, provided with a matching control trailer and, in 1977, appeared in service in silver livery and aptly named *Silver Jubilee*. It had very considerable teething troubles but proved useful enough to survive and has since undergone various metamorphoses; it seems to be the 'pet' unit which Ravenglass Works apparently needs, to have a love/hate relationship with! For the 1984 Liverpool Festival it was reborn as a two power-car, two trailer set with one semi-open trailer and a closed one fitted for disabled passengers. The ensemble was painted in BR intercity colours which it retained in 1987, though the trailers appeared to spend most of their time running as normal coaches.

The major addition to the stud was undoubtedly a railway-designed diesel main line locomotive built at Ravenglass in 1979-80. A double-bogie machine with torque-converter drive and a single, end cab, it came into service in mid-1980, being appropriately named *Lady Wakefield*; it was painted maroon with relieving trim.

As regards the coaching stock, there was a massive transformation during the period, probably greater than at any other time in the railway's history. Certainly by 1966 most of the wooden stock was over thirty years old and, living largely in the open, was nearing the end of its life. A twofold programme of renewal was therefore undertaken. Existing opens were largely replaced with locally-built 20-seaters using salvageable seat units, while a policy of steady acquisition of new aluminium bodied closed coaches was begun. Based on the Myers and Bowman type, these were built by Edmund Crow of Cleator Moor and by 1982 some seventeen fully-enclosed and eight semi-open vehicles were in use. It is pleasant to record that one of the last decisions of Lord Wakefield's reign was the production of three semi-opens specifically fitted for carriage of disabled passengers, a facility which sees regular use.

TRACKS AND BUILDINGS

Up to 1968, the railway had trundled quietly along, refurbishing itself slowly from fairly small resources—the constraints may be shown by the fact that it was not until 1967 that the last of the long sleepers on the old mixed gauge section were replaced. The new management embarked on a much needed programme of complete track renewal that extended into the 1980s, using largely new rail from Workington and consignments of Jarrah hardwood sleepers from Australia; these may have been an expensive investment but have laid the foundations for many years of good running. The result was that, by the time recession arrived, the majority of track was in better shape than it had, perhaps, ever been. Additionally the more rational operating methods described above were introduced, leading to the progressive signalling of Ravenglass station, using semaphores operated from a lever frame and interlocked with main points.

Major expenditure on the track was only a start. The new regime had considerable experience in obtaining grants from various bodies for improvements likely to enhance the local environment, and full use has been made of these in developing the railway's amenities—albeit considerable capital expenditures were also required and accepted. Consequently, and unusually for the Ratty, the development of physical plant has taken place in stages rather than in the previous 'grand clear-out' manner.

As one might expect, most of the visible building modifications took place in and around Ravenglass. The first major one was installation, in 1968–9, of the neat wooden signalbox. It was followed in 1970 by erection of a diesel locomotive shed at the north end of the loco sidings, a much needed amenity which has become more and more vital with continued expansion of the locomotive fleet. There was then a considerable pause while the company turned covetous eyes on its big next-door neighbour which had decided to make Ravenglass BR into an unstaffed halt. Sundry negotiations took place and eventually all main BR buildings changed hands. The old BR signalbox became a company sanctum, and sometime boardroom, while the erstwhile goods shed was used as a store and workshop. The main down-line buildings were screened off from their platform and, in 1976, became a company pub, the 'Ratty Arms', which serves both drinks and an extensive range of bar meals. It quickly became popular with tourist and locals alike, and is now an attraction in its own right. It was followed, in 1977 by acquisition of the big up-line platform shelter, the R & E R providing a new mini-shelter in part-exchange. The goods shed, which had housed a centenary exhibition was now converted to a proper joiners shop and the shelter, greatly extended and modified, became home to the Railway Museum.

Meanwhile, the rather unimpressive passenger facilities of Ravenglass R & E R station were also being transformed. With a grant from the English Tourist Board, an imposing Victorian platform awning from Millom was erected on the west side in 1971-2 and backed by a sandstone and roughcast wall. It provided cover for three roads and platforms two and three. In 1979-80 a new two-storey office and toilet block was inserted between a refettled teabar and the bungalow and four years later the ensemble was completed by erection of a wood and metal awning over platform one. With a general tidying up and improvement to surrounding grass areas, the station then looked very attractive indeed. It was further enhanced in 1982-3 when a new stone and slate building was constructed near the old booking office to house both a covered booking hall for the railway and an excellent tourist information office for the district. Operationally the station was improved by tarmacing the carpark, erecting an automatic coach washing machine down by the goods shed and by putting in permanent rail access to the museum.

This is probably also the place to mention in some detail two developments which are managed by the railway even if not strictly railway property. These are the railway museum previously mentioned and Muncaster Water Mill. To ensure their independent continuance and, no doubt, to increase their potential for grant aid, these were established under the guidance of a non-profit making body, the Eskdale (Cumbria) Trust, which in turn delegates their operation to the railway company. The museum is, of course, intimately connected in that its exhibits are largely railway-owned and railway staff are seconded to maintain it. Muncaster Mill which has, by considerable effort, been restored from near dereliction to full working order, has its own miller and provides both an additional point of interest and some additional traffic for the railway.

MAJOR HISTORICAL EVENTS

What then, of the railway's general events and incidents while all these developments were taking place? There have been plenty which could be recorded, from involvement with a resuscitated Ravenglass Fair each Whitsun, to such oddities as sponsored coach pushes but a list would probably bring nostalgia only to those actually having taken part. The railway tries to put on something different each year, if only for the publicity.

Perhaps the most interesting events from the railway enthusiast's point of view were the long (and no doubt continuing) series of locomotive visits and exchanges initiated by a direct parallel with the 1920s. RH & DR No 2 *Northern Chief*, second of the original Greenly pacifics, came to Ravenglass in 1971 like his sister earlier, to show what such a machine could do on the Ravenglass road and to provide comparison trials of such things as superheat and springing; in what was also to become a tradition, a Romney driver, Terry Whawell, came with the locomotive to ensure all went smoothly and the trials were watched with great interest by many in the 15 inch gauge world. They certainly influenced the design of *Northern Rock*. More interestingly, perhaps, they also started a whole series of motive power exchanges between Romney and Ravenglass—some for serious reasons, some more for fun than anything else. Thus, from the RH & D, No 10, *Doctor Syn*, came up for the centenary in 1976 (see below); No 8 *Hurricane* visited in 1981 and one of the 4–8–2s *Hercules* spent three weeks in service in 1986 (strictly outside this period but it fits here!). RH & DR No 11 *Black Prince*, a comparatively recent acquisition from Germany, even spent most of a season working regularly out of Ravenglass in 1982, substituting for *Shelagh of Eskdale* which had gone to 'prove' diesel traction on the Romney line. Equally, R & E R locos have regularly gone south, *River Mite* joining *Shelagh* for a short period and both *Lady Wakefield* and *Synolda* put in appearances there while, later in 1985, *River Esk* visited as well. Whether one includes in this category *River Irt's* sojourn in York Museum for the Heywood celebrations is not so clear!

There have also, usually concurrently with the above visits, been what can only be called mass descents by visiting locomotives which are noted in the appropriate places below. The most important have probably been those intended to celebrate major anniversaries. Perhaps two stand out particularly. In 1976 the Ratty officially celebrated 100 years of life as a passenger railway and the year was certainly memorable. A special photo album, 'Ratty's 100' was commissioned; an elaborate exhibition of the line's history was staged in the old goods shed throughout the season and, on an appropriate weekend, there was a grand fiesta with staff and visitors dressed in period costume, and special workings to a centenary feast at Dalegarth. Later in the year there was something for the enthusiasts with a gathering of locomotives which saw a veritable procession from Dalegarth to Ravenglass. Five years later, in 1981, the Preservation

Society celebrated its 21st birthday with another round of junketings and an even more elaborate cavalcade with engines from all over the place.

A DIVERSIFICATION OF ACTIVITIES

Lord Wakefield died in 1983 but his family continued the business and the R & E R is still very much a going concern at the time of writing. If there is a change it is more of a shift of emphasis. Even before 1983 it was clear that the market for tourist railways was not going to expand for ever; traffic peaked in 1978. After that, the proliferation of tourist attractions in the Lake District, and the increase in cost of petrol, then caused a decline in numbers until 1985. It is fair to say that recession brought a drop in tourists generally as many of the traditional customers drew in their horns and matters were not helped by the series of media scares about Sellafield at that time. Hence, while developing its passenger business so far as conditions allowed, the railway company was asked also to diversify so as to utilise its resources to the full.

The most obvious potential source of income was to use the existing physical plant and technical expertise to take on engineering work for outside customers. A fairly tentative attempt to rescue the manufacture of Clupet piston rings did not prove fruitful—it did not fit in with work patterns. On the other hand Ravenglass Works has successfully tendered for overhauls ranging from industrial diesels to one of the massive 21-inch gauge Hudswell Clarke machines from Blackpool Pleasure Beach. It has also built new machines, first a vertical boilered tram for a friend of the railway and then a 12-inch gauge version of *Lady Wakefield* for the Ruislip Lido railway.

The railway also set out to sell its operating expertise. Increasingly, promoters of major tourist attractions in this country and overseas perceive that a large-scale miniature railway can be an important part of their schemes. The R & E R and R H & D R are without doubt the pre-eminent operators of such railways and their advice and help is clearly proving useful.

As to further general developments, the complete renewal of track, with new materials, has been slowed down but should be finished by 1991-2. A new generation of maximum loading-gauge, 24-seat coaches is being designed for production in 1988 and promise to set a new standard of comfort for the 15-inch gauge. The Wakefield family appears to be just as interested in the continuance of the railway as was Lord Wakefield himself and, so far as such things can be in an ever changing world, its future seems assured.

CHAPTER 9

3 ft Gauge Equipment

LOCOMOTIVES

Manning, Wardle 0-6-0T's 545/75 *Devon and* 629/76 *Nab Gill*

To work the goods traffic when the line was first opened, a single locomotive was ordered from Manning, Wardle Limited of Leeds, being delivered at the end of May 1875. It was a six-coupled machine of a standard design supplied to many contractors and minor railways but, as can be seen from Fig 1, was unusual for a Manning, Wardle in having side tanks instead of a saddle tank.

For the first year, *Devon* (presumably named after the Earl of Devon) handled all traffic but was joined by a similar machine during the summer of 1876. These two handled all work on the line for the remainder of its existence. For some reason they always worked facing down the valley, an odd fact when one considers that most adverse grades were in the opposite direction.

There are no definite records of any major repairs except for a 'rebuild' of *Devon* by Lowca in the 1890s although both were maintained by fitters from the Furness Railway when needed, and on occasions were sent to the FR's Moor Row shops if the facilities at Ravenglass were insufficient. *Nab Gill* appears to have been in poor condition by the early 1900s, only being used as spare engine and apparently becoming unserviceable about 1905. There is a reference to one engine 'being off for several weeks receiving a thorough overhaul' in 1905, and it is probable that *Devon* was fettled up for further use; no doubt the company could not afford thoroughly to repair two locomotives. Certainly *Devon* was the only locomotive in use after 1908 and the fate of both is unknown for certain. Tradition has it that they were cut up on site in 1915 and the bits taken away by rail. Livery in the early days was lined green with the name transferred on to the tank sides and the initials R & ER in

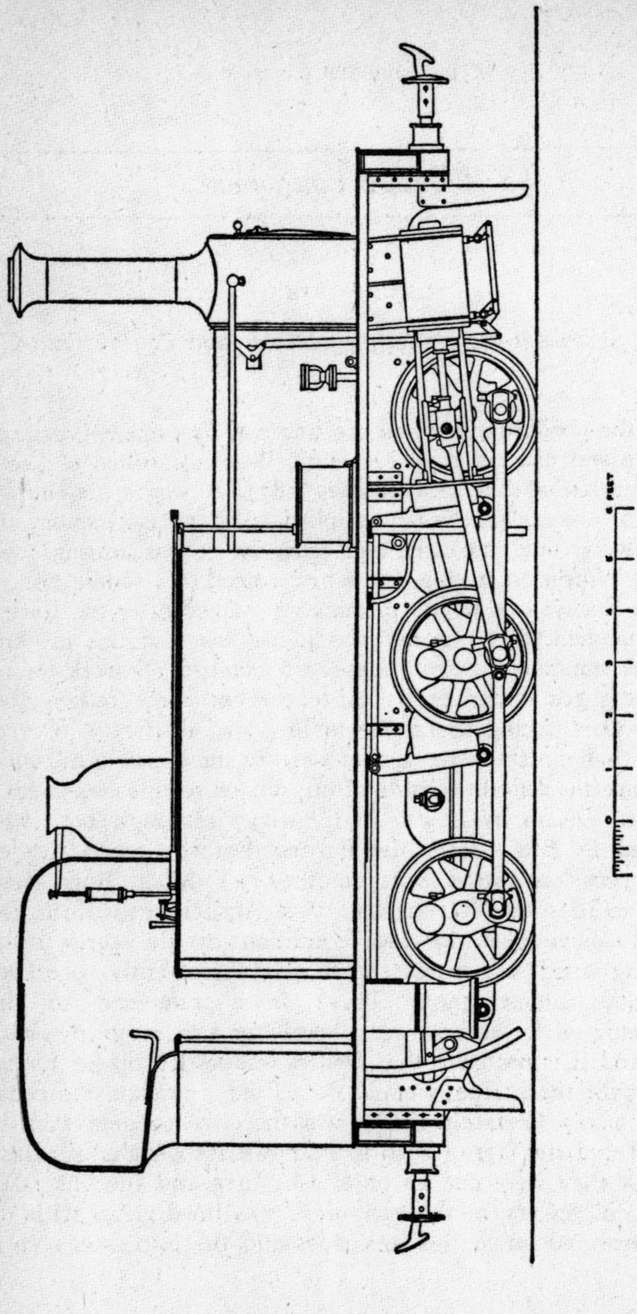

(3) *Manning Wardle 3 ft gauge* 0–6–0T

transfers on the front buffer beam. *Nab Gill* later was in plain green or black without name, and *Devon* may have been re-painted likewise. An old hand-tinted card shows the locomotive black and a coach in varnished brown but the accuracy of this cannot be established.

Dimensions were as follows: Gauge 3 ft; Length over beams 9 ft 1 in; Width overall 6 ft 8 in; Height to cab 6 ft 4 in; Wheelbase 9 ft 7 in; Wheel dia (on tread) 2 ft 9 in; Cyls—dia 10 in; Cyls—stroke 16 in; Heating surface 297 sq ft; Working pressure 160 psi.

COACHES

For the opening of the line, the R & E bought two compartment coaches and a four-wheel brake van. The maker was the Bristol Wagon Company, but no drawings survive and the vehicles did not last long enough to be measured by any enthusiast. The following notes should identify them. One was a first class coach, the other a third class one, second class apparently never being provided though all trains were advertised on early timetables as first, second and third class.

First class coach. This was a three-compartment, four-wheeler of conventional appearance, with side doors and transverse seating. Louvre ventilators were provided above the door droplights and each compartment was lit by a Colza oil lamp in the roof—although to judge from photographs showing a solitary lamp housing in position, only one of the three was regularly lit! No doubt first class traffic was not very brisk on winter evenings and, in later years, the coach was used as a composite. The body was of wood with plywood or matchboard panelling and mounted on a steel underframe with laminated spring axleboxes. Double footboards were fitted, small individual upper ones above a long step. Construction was fairly light and the bodywork deteriorated somewhat in later years.

Third class coach. This was similar in construction and dimensions to the first class vehicle, but had narrower compartments and a coupé compartment for the guard at its 'Boot' end. The three compartments had three-quarter height partitions and were lighted by two lamps. These were rather subtly placed, the guard having most of the benefit from one, which was placed over the 'partition' between his compartment and the next, while the rest had to make do with one placed centrally over the middle compartment.

Both these coaches survived until 1915 at least, being stored on the old loading bank after gauge conversions. They are said to have been bought by a local farmer and taken away on road wagons.

Brake van. This was a four-wheel vehicle with a 'bird-cage' lookout at the Ravenglass end, vaguely resembling those then used on the Furness Railway. It had a single sliding door in each side and separate door with droplight for the guard. The lookout was peculiar in having windows overlooking only the roof; to look sideways or to the rear the guard had to stick his head out of the door or use a small window set centrally in the back bulkhead of the van. The underframe appears to have been identical with those of the coaches.

The van was used on all trains and is believed to have ended its days as a platelayer's hut just above what is now the site of Murthwaite Halt, probably about 1912.

The 'big saloon'. Almost as soon as the line opened, it was obvious that seating capacity would be insufficient at peak periods, and Mr Quan had built at Ravenglass a large and somewhat crude four-wheel coach. It was no less than 22 ft 6 in long and had a timber-framed body with small windows right round it, high up in the body side, and a single door in the centre of each side. Seats were arranged all round the perimeter with an additional ottoman-type bench in the centre. The whole thing was spartan in the extreme. It was intended simply as a large-capacity vehicle for peak traffic and workmen's trains, gaining the soubriquet 'cattle truck' from the way in which passengers were packed in on these occasions.

After closure, the coach was stored at Ravenglass until 1915 and then sold locally. It survived until 1965 as a shed, latterly beside the main-line railway bridge at Ravenglass. Part is still extant in a garden. Dimensions of body were 22 ft 6 in long, 7 ft 1 in wide, and 6 ft 6 in inside height.

WAGONS

There appear from photographs to have been three varieties of four-wheel wagons in use, two being bought from Bristol and the other made locally.

Side-door wagons. Photographs show two varieties of these on similar underframes with laminated-spring axleboxes. One has a two-plank body with dropsides and the other has higher, three-plank sides and ends with centre drop-doors. Both types were used for general traffic and were also used as overflow passenger vehicles, garden seats being placed longitudinally along each side, facing inwards. The total number is unknown but was certainly small, probably not exceeding six; it may not have exceeded the four (two of each type) shown in some photographs.

Ore wagons. About thirty short, four-wheel wagons were built locally at Mr Quan's instance for the ore traffic. No dimensions survive, but they had box-like three-plank bodies raised from the underframes by transverse timber baulks. They had provision for tipping to the north side only. Frames were of timber, with simple cast axleboxes and spoked wheels. The survivors are said to have been burned in 1915.

CHAPTER 10

15 in Gauge Steam Locomotives

THE SCALE MODELS

Sans Pareil, the first locomotive brought to Ravenglass by NGR Limited was, as might be expected, a Bassett-Lowke product. It was a scale model 4–4–2 tender locomotive of that firm's '30' Class 'Improved Little Giant' design. In spite of the fact that only three or four were built the '30' Class have caused so much confusion to enthusiasts that the history of this particular example must be recounted in detail.

The history of *Sans Pareil* (a Mitchell-bestowed name) is not clear, several authorities, including the designer, Henry Greenly, having stated that it was built in 1912 for an exhibition line at Geneva and afterwards lay dormant at the Bassett-Lowke works until the Eskdale scheme provided a new lease of life. It arrived at Ravenglass in a large packing-case clearly marked 'Geneva Miniature Railway'.

It is also on record that the locomotive was formerly named *Prins Olaf* and that a '30' Class locomotive of that name had been built in 1913 for an exhibition line run by NGR Limited at Cristiania (now Oslo) in Norway. The *Whitehaven News* of 2 September 1915 recording the opening of the line, states that 'Mr J. Wills...was in Cristiania with this identical engine and part of this rolling stock' and this ties in closely with local recollections. *Prins Olaf,* too, is a name more likely to be commemorating a Norwegian venture than a Swiss one. It therefore seems certain that *Sans Pareil* came from Oslo via Northampton and that she arrived in the misleading packing-case probably because it happened to be conveniently on hand at the time. As a tailpiece, she was No 31, the second of the class to be built (a photograph taken at Oslo shows this clearly) so it is not at all unlikely that she went first to Geneva, then to Oslo and then on to Ravenglass!

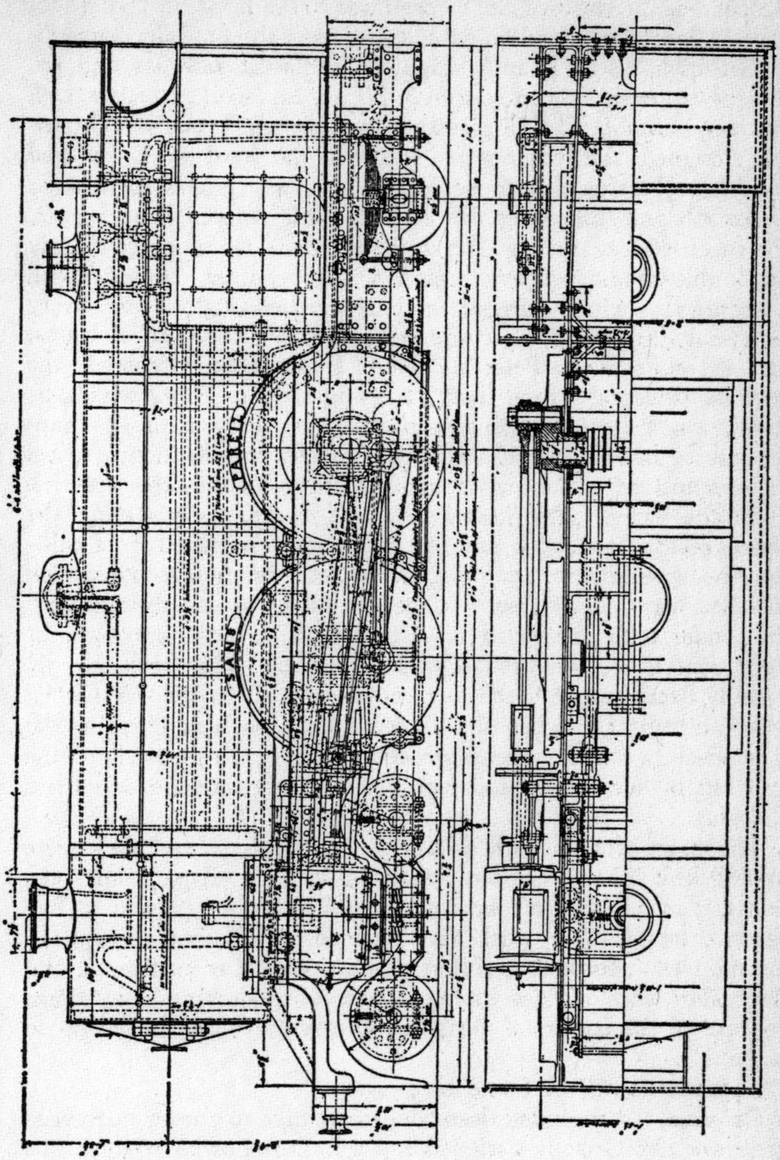

(4a) Sans Pareil

Whatever her history, *Sans Pareil* was a standard 3 in to-the-foot scale 'Atlantic' of Class '30' which was itself the final development of Greenly's 'Little Giant' design for miniature railways and the general arrangement can be seen in Fig 4a. An excellent scale model, and very suitable for the pleasure lines for which she was originally designed, she was not really up to the hard work involved once heavy trains had to be hauled up steep grades to Boot or Dalegarth and, following the arrival of *Sir Aubrey Brocklebank*, she was used less and less. Her duties in later days consisted mainly in double-heading heavy trains when required, usually with *Colossus* (for which purpose she changed her original blue livery to a matching red one); running light specials and relief trains; and driver-training. Peter Le Neve Foster recalls that all the 'express' drivers got their initial training on *Sans Pareil* which, he states, was a very sweet engine to drive and easy to fire, perhaps because of her shorter firebox. She also had the distinctive wheel reverser instead of the lever reverser fitted to all the other engines.

By the early 1920s *Sans Pareil* was undoubtedly feeling the effects of too-hard work and her decline was hastened by a collision in the summer of 1920 or 1921 with the original scooter which smashed her tender frame. For the rest of the season she ran with the tender body supported on a flat truck, a rather incongruous sight, but it was repaired during the winter. The work she did steadily decreased, and the last known date on which she worked was Whitsun 1926 when she hauled a four-coach relief train. She was officially withdrawn at the end of the 1926 season and the best bits of her wheels and running gear were used to patch up *Colossus*.

The main trouble with all the scale models is that they were overworked. They were too lightly built, with all parts to scale, and this meant that all wearing parts had to be renewed at frequent intervals. The work also strained the frames unduly, all locomotives at some time suffering from cracked main frames, and the boilers wore out, developing bulged tubeplates and leaky seams because of the continual sustained efforts they were called on to make.

Dimensions will be found on p 130.

Colossus, the second scale-model locomotive to appear at Ravenglass was also Greenly-designed and a Bassett-Lowke product. She was also acquired by NGR Limited at second-hand, having been built as the *John Anthony* for Captain J. E. P. Howey's private railway at Staughton Manor.

Page 115: LAST DAYS OF THE HEYWOODS

[*above*] *Old scene: 'Ella', collecting wagons of stone.* [*below*] *Power for the drills: 'Muriel' on a flat wagon*

Page 116: MORE TRACTORS

[*above*] *The first version of ICL No 1 at speed with a light train.* [*below*] *ICL No 2 (rebuilt 'Ella') having test train of twenty wagons at Murthwaite*

She was in effect a simple elongation of the '30' Class 'Atlantic' with an extra pair of coupled wheels added to make her a 4–6–2. She was illustrated in Bassett-Lowke's literature as the '60' or 'Gigantic' Class. Apart from the longer boiler, dimensions were similar to those of the 'Atlantic' as was the appearance. As with *Sans Pareil* an eight-wheel bogie tender was fitted, the locomotive being 'true-scale' to British loading gauge.

At Ravenglass, *Colossus* put in a tremendous amount of hard work, sharing the main passenger duties with *Sans Pareil* and then with *Sir Aubrey*. As with the other scale models she was too lightly built and suffered a number of mishaps in service, including the breaking of a driving axle. When Beckfoot Quarry opened in 1922 she had to be fitted with extra sanding gear to act as a standby for the Heywoods and for working general goods trains. Page 58 shows the neat prolongation of the front running plate, a modification apparently carried out at Ravenglass, on which the sand boxes were fixed. The extension disappeared in 1925, when on a March morning she met *Muriel* head-on beneath the bridge at Eskdale Green station.

Muriel escaped with badly-damaged drawgear but *Colossus* had her buffer beam wrapped round the cylinders and badly-twisted frames which proved hard to straighten out. She had a complete overhaul before she emerged again in time for the 1926 season, sporting a massive wooden front buffer-beam to strengthen her front end. It was probably the enforced 'rest' which enabled her to work right up to the end of the 1927 season instead of being retired with *Sans Pareil*. She was withdrawn from service officially in November 1927 and scrapped immediately, her chassis and running gear being re-used in the construction of the first *River Mite*. Dimensions will be found on p 130.

Sir Aubrey Brocklebank, third and last of the true scale-model locomotives to be used on the R & E, was the final development of Greenly's 'Little Giant—Gigantic' chain of design. She was, in effect, a 'super-gigantic', the main improvements being a slightly larger boiler pitched higher in the frames, which brought her height near to the (scale) continental loading gauge, Greenly's smokebox 'superheater'—in reality a gridiron steam drier, and a six-wheel tender. Otherwise, dimensions are similar to *Colossus* and it is believed that *Sans Pareil* drawings were used.

As with other R & E equipment of this period, *Sir Aubrey*'s history is odd. To begin with, there was considerable argument over who designed her; W. V. Cauchi claimed to have done so, but he

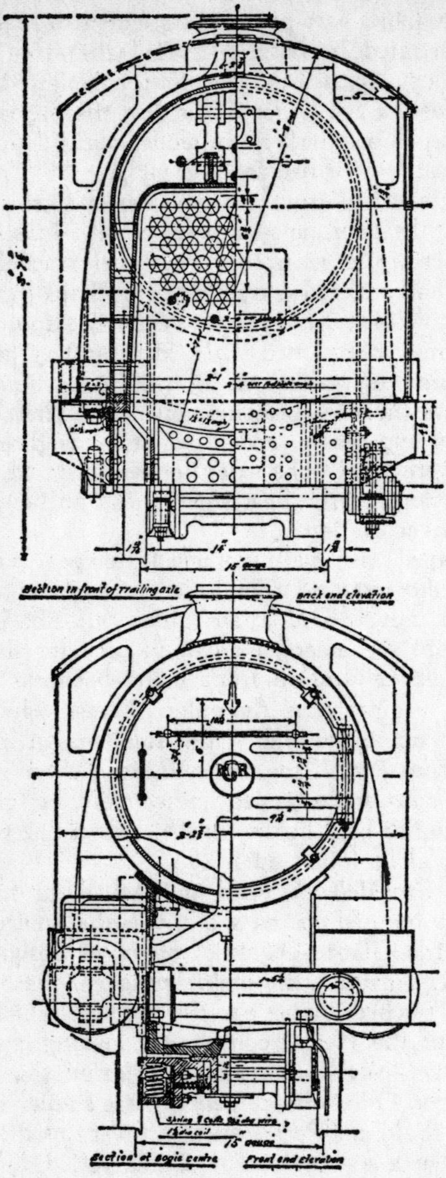

(4b) *End views of* Sans Pareil *and* Colossus

probably did little more than specify the larger boiler and make detail modifications to Greenly's design. Secondly, she was not built by Bassett-Lowke, which on first consideration seems odd as Bassett-Lowke himself was still very much involved with the line. The probable explanation is that Bassett-Lowke was full up with war work when the order was placed and that Cauchi had connections with the small Bournemouth light engineering firm of Hunt & Company, which was given the job.

Whatever the reason, the R & E had no reason to be dissatisfied. *Sir Aubrey* was the first and only locomotive that Hunts built and they made a very good job of it; it is still remembered with pride in the works. The boiler was sub-contracted to a now-unknown firm, and brass castings were brought in from Smith, Dorman & Company. Otherwise, all work was done by Hunt.

Sir Aubrey proved welcome reinforcement for the hard-pressed motive power department and, as the 'new engine', undoubtedly took a major share of the work. She suffered from the same light build as the other scale models, indeed actually breaking her frame in 1926, and she had an additional defect which it would appear should be blamed on Cauchi's design influence. Her firebox, instead of having the usual foundation ring, had its inner box and outer shell tapered together at the base. The uneven expansion caused much distortion and cracking, and no real cure for the trouble was ever found.

When she arrived on the line her livery was light blue, but this was changed to Midland Red, lined gold and white, for the 1925 season and changed again the following year to green. She was withdrawn along with *Colossus* in 1927 for the same reasons. Her chassis was used complete under the front part of the first *River Mite*.

It may be of interest to quote the normal end-of-season repairs carried out to *Sir Aubrey* in 1926 to show what punishment the scale-models took. Engine (i.e. mechanical) repairs: back frame stretcher casting repaired; running boards welded where necessary; cab welded where necessary; buffer beam straightened; exhaust pipe joints re-made; bogie pin and side springs renewed; various bearings re-bushed. *Boiler* (re-tubed 1/26); Firebox seams caulked. all round; firebox welded on all four corners and two inside back seams. *Tender*: Side frames straightened; new wheels and axles; new hanger bars all round.

Dimensions will be found on p 130.

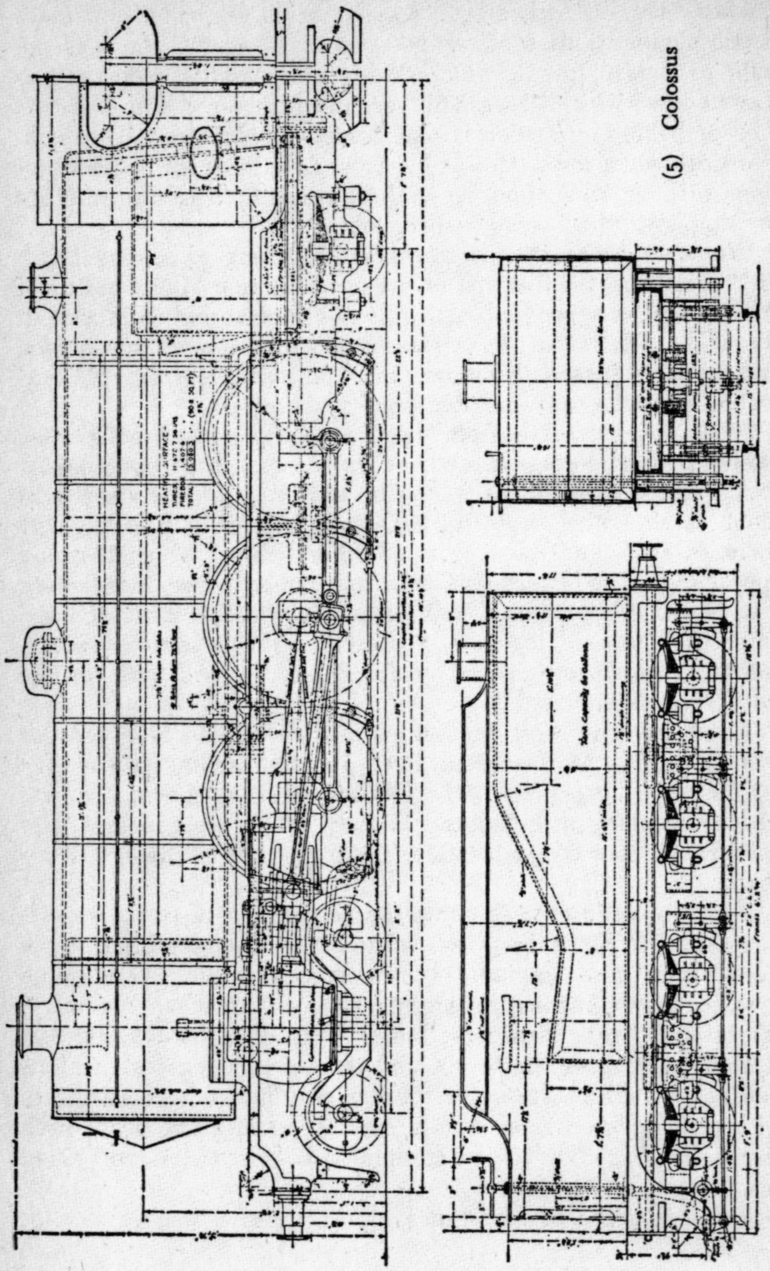

(5) Colossus

THE HEYWOOD SISTERS

The Heywood Sisters. During 1916 and 1917, the R & E purchased three of the six 15 in gauge locomotives built by Sir A. P. Heywood. All were already well-worn, having been constructed during the 1880s and 1890s, and comprised his Nos 2 and 3 from Duffield Bank and his No 4 from Eaton Hall, where it had been replaced by two more powerful 0–6–0T's.

All three were built to Heywood's ideas of utilising maximum loading gauge and were true narrow gauge locomotives, not miniatures. They were all cabless, side-tank engines, Heywood's dictum on cabs being that 'a stout mackintosh is both cheaper and far better for the driver'! All had pinnace-type boilers with cylindrical fireboxes, inevitably following his other dicta that (i) all wheels should be coupled to provide maximum adhesion; (ii) there should be an equal overhang front and rear. In service, these theories had their flaws, especially on the Eskdale line, where long, hard hauls overtaxed the limited steaming capacity of the boilers and the bitter Eskdale weather sorely tried the exposed drivers. It is greatly to the credit of Heywood's design and construction that the locomotives lasted as long as they did. Brief notes appear below.

Heywood No 2 0–6–0T Ella. Completed in 1881, *Ella* was the first locomotive to embody all Sir Arthur's theories and to incorporate his patent radial gear for easing the rigid wheelbase on sharp curves. She was built for the demonstration line at Duffield Bank and put in a considerable amount of work before going to Eskdale. There she worked hard until the mid 1920s and was evidently a popular engine, for at various times suggestions were made that she should be oil-fired and, in 1927, a plan was drawn up (Fig 9) for converting her to petrol-electric drive. In 1922 or 1923 her firebox was damaged as described in Chapter VI and, by the time the new régime took over, it was obvious that she needed a complete re-boilering. She was therefore dismantled and her frames and wheels used to construct ICL No 2.

Heywood No 3 0–8–0T Muriel. Built in 1894, *Muriel* was Heywood's favourite locomotive and was frequently used to demonstrate that a 15 in gauge machine could haul heavy loads. She seems to have been more badly worn than *Ella* on arrival in Eskdale and, during the early 1920s, was used less and less. She was withdrawn after the 1926 season and, after a few months acting

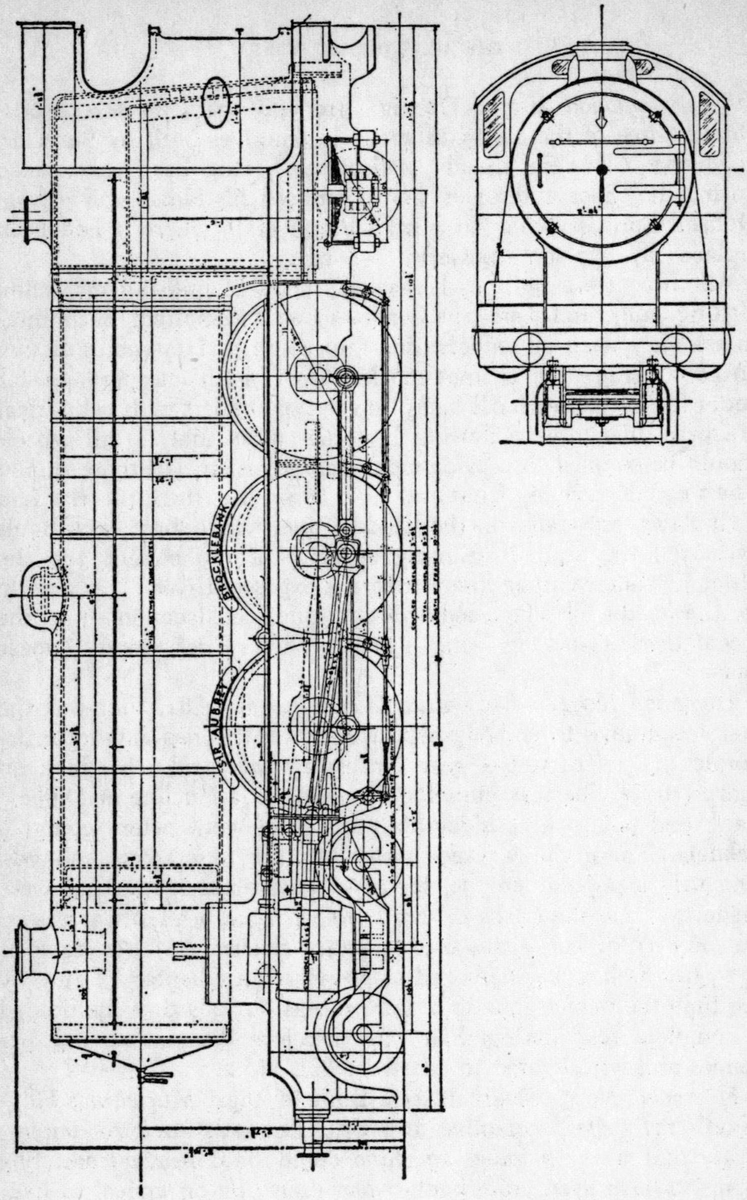

(6) Sir Aubrey Brocklebank

as stationary boiler at Beckfoot Quarry, was stripped down for conversion into *River Irt*.

Heywood No 4 0–4–0T *Katie*. *Katie* was built in 1896 specifically for the Duke of Westminster's estate railway which Heywood

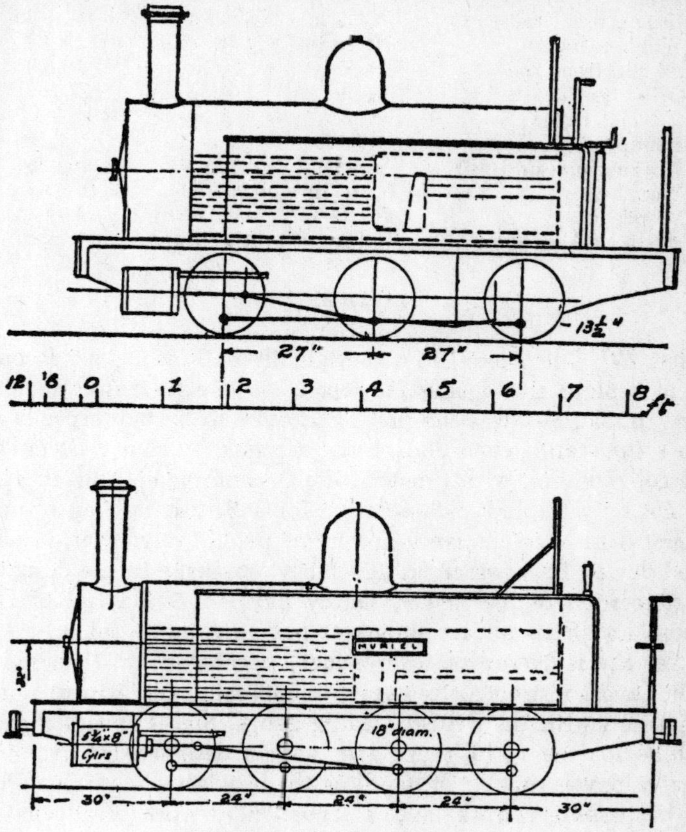

(7) *The Heywood locomotives*

was then constructing at Eaton Hall. Heywood stated that she was built as an experiment, to see if a small four-coupled locomotive could do the work required, and he confessed that she was not altogether successful, being hard on the track. None the less, she was worked very hard and was badly worn when she came to Eskdale—the R & E must have been fairly desperate to buy her. The long runs of the R & E also showed up the limited steaming capacity of her small boiler and she was very soon retired to Irton Road shed as spare engine. After the arrival of *Sir Aubrey* in 1919 she was sold to the Llewellyn Miniature Railway at Southport.

Dimension	*Ella*	*Muriel*	*Katie*
Type	0–6–0T	0–8–0T	0–4–0T
Length over headstocks	8 ft 8 in	10 ft 9 in	8 ft 0 in
Width overall	3 ft 10 in	3 ft 10 in	3 ft 10 in
Height from rail	N/K	N/K	N/K
Cylinders dia	$4\frac{7}{8}$ in	$6\frac{1}{4}$ in	$4\frac{5}{8}$ in
stroke	7 in	8 in	7 in
Heating surface	70 sq/ft	91 sq/ft	53 sq/ft
Working pressure (psi)	160 lb	160 lb	160 lb
Wheelbase	4 ft 6 in	6 ft 0 in	3 ft 0 in
Wheel dia	1 ft $1\frac{1}{2}$ in	1 ft 6 in	1 ft 3 in
Wt in working order	3 t 15 c	5 t 0 c	3 t 5 c

RIVER ESK

River Esk. The *River Esk* was originally built as a goods locomotive to replace the ageing Heywoods on the increasingly heavy quarry traffic. She was the first locomotive to be built specifically for R & E operating conditions, being designed by Henry Greenly in close collaboration with Proctor Mitchell and, when built in 1923, was not only the first 2–8–2 design for a British railway but also the first British locomotive to use Lentz poppet valve gear, suitably scaled down. This was fitted at a fairly late stage in the design at the suggestion of the maker, Davey Paxman & Co Ltd of Colchester, and from all accounts was not very successful.

River Esk is overall of scale-model appearance but freelance in outline and constructed to a scale of approximately 4 in to 1 ft in comparison with the British loading gauge. She is thus a massive machine for the 15 in gauge and, with a designed tractive effort of 2,100 lb, was capable of handling the heaviest stone trains. Pressure of passenger work, and a tendency to work erratically restricted her use and, when the new régime took over early in 1925, she was standing sheeted up in the back of the shed. It was found that her driving wheels were badly balanced and they were replaced by a new set before trials re-commenced in the spring of 1925. The main source of trouble was the Lentz gear and, although modifications to this made her freer running, her beat was always somewhat erratic.

The management decided early in 1927 to have her rebuilt with Walschaerts gear and at the same time to convert her to the Poultney articulated system with an additional power unit under

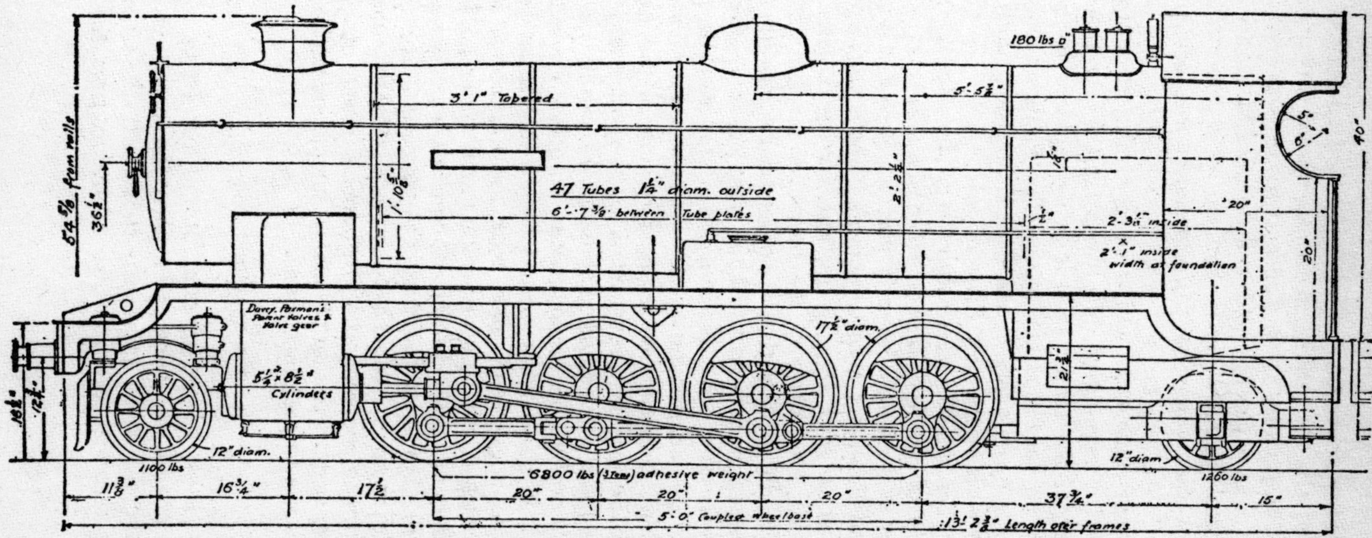

(8) River Esk – *side elevation*

the tender. The conversion was authorised on 16 March, and she was taken to the Yorkshire Engine Company for modification, returning on 12 January 1928. The next month was occupied with trials to cure steaming deficiencies and defective feedwater arrangements, the trials culminating in haulage of 34 tons of stone on 15 February—after which she was pronounced satisfactory and put into service.

The Poultney conversion, with a wheel arrangement of 2–8–2 + 0–8–0, proved disappointing and was scrapped over the weekend 9-11 June 1931, the tender chassis being replaced by two four-wheel bogies on hardwood mountings. The Poultney chassis itself languished for many years in the back fitting shop until used in 1964 for the basis of the new *River Mite*.

River Esk then ran very successfully on goods and passenger trains until the end of the 1939 season, when she was put in store for the duration of the war. The early post-war period was a time of shortages and *River Esk* needed renewal of some parts, so was not steamed until 20 May 1952, going into service that season. She has since been a mainstay of the passenger services and is kept in excellent condition. As with all the other locomotives still working, she has been regularly overhauled and refettled, components being replaced as necessary. She was reboilered in 1983 using the railway's standard boiler—a derivation of the original one for *River Esk*. Her original boiler, incidentally, is preserved for museum use. Advantage was taken of the need for a new firebox to incorporate some of L. D. Porta's ideas for improved fuel combustion. The result is impressive and certainly enables the locomotive to burn low grade fuel very effectively... In more minor matters, a new tender has been built using the old bogies and since 1968 the locomotive has been blackberry-black with an approximation to LNWR lining. It may be of interest that, in 1926, oil-firing experiments were carried out on *River Esk* with a burner of Ted Wright's own design. They were not persisted with as no cure could be found for the leaking tubes caused by rapid warming and cooling of the burners. These, of course, cut out whenever steam was shut off and the undulating nature of Ratty meant that was a frequent occurrence.

R & E R REBUILDS

River Irt. Even in her present form, *River Irt* can probably claim to be one of the oldest 15 in gauge locomotives in these islands. As several writers, apparently struck with the same flash of poesy, have recorded, she 'rose like a phoenix from the ashes of

Muriel'...which rather overstates the matter as in essence she IS *Muriel*.

What happened was that, while *Muriel*'s boiler was worn out, her frames and running gear were perfectly sound. It was therefore decided to rebuild her with a scale-model type boiler, at the same time lengthening the frames by 2 ft 6 in to allow the fitting of a trailing axle, thus making her into an 0–8–2. The Yorkshire Engine Company supplied a boiler, the rest of the work being carried out at Ravenglass during the early summer of 1927. Steaming trials were carried out in July and she entered revenue service on 1 August, an appropriate builder's plate being affixed to the cab side. Nameplates were not added until the following year.

The conversion proved very successful, the locomotive-type boiler being without the steaming defects characteristic of Heywood boilers, while the trailing wheels needed for carrying the deeper firebox also steadied the locomotive and greatly reduced the 'hunting' to which all Heywood locomotives were susceptible. Aesthetically, it was not so good since the combination of scale-model fittings and *Muriel*'s wide running plate have produced a rather squat locomotive with little protection for the driver.

River Irt has worked mainly on passenger trains. She was the first locomotive to be steamed after the war ended and since then has been used extensively. A new firebox was fitted in the winter of 1962-3, together with a steam brake. Increasingly, however, the railway management was dissatisfied with her hybrid appearance and, in 1971-2, she was drastically altered to give a narrow gauge outline with tall funnel and dome, and a much higher and larger cab. The result, while not entirely aesthetically pleasing owing mainly to cab design, is certainly a great improvement on her previous state. She was equipped with a new bogie tender in 1972 and reboilered in 1978, since which she has continued to run as reliably as ever. She spent most of the 1984 season at Liverpool.

River Mite (1). The first *River Mite* built at Ravenglass during the winter of 1927-8, was an ingenious attempt to obtain a cheap but powerful articulated locomotive. It will be recalled that the original three 'scale models' had similar engines and running gear and, after withdrawal of *Colossus* and *Sir Aubrey* in November 1927, their frames and running gear were thoroughly overhauled, the rear portions of each with the trailing wheels being discarded to leave two 4–6–0 chassis. Certain spare parts from *Sans Pareil* were incorporated in these.

The Yorkshire Engine Company then supplied a large boiler,

with Belpaire firebox, sufficiently large to supply the needs of four cylinders, and a tenderbody and cab were fabricated at Ravenglass. The whole superstructure was then mounted on heavy, well-shaped sideframes of ¾ in-plate steel, bolted to the tender sides and to a saddle under the centre of the boiler barrel. The arrangement can clearly be seen on page 98. The front chassis unit was pivoted from this saddle on a rigid pin and the rear one was pivoted on a similar pin fixed to a plate under the tender. Each unit had its own built-up saddles to provide bearing surfaces, one beneath the pivot pin and one above the cylinders in each case. The latter mounting could slide laterally to provide articulation, the boiler or tender being supported by bearing plates.

Steam was supplied to the cylinders by flexible jointed pipes; the exhaust from the rear unit went into and through a feedwater heater on the tendertank.

All work was carried out during the early part of 1928, between 3 January and 9 April, the first trial run being on 12 April. The locomotive went into traffic on Whit Monday.

In service, the new locomotive proved powerful and was used on both stone and passenger trains, but the frame structure proved inadequate to cope with the considerable stresses set up by heavy loads. The old scale models' frames had always been weak and it appears that the rigid method of articulation aggravated their weakness. The chassis tended to distort badly under load and the locomotive eventually became unsafe to work. She was therefore withdrawn at the end of the 1937 season and partly dismantled, with the intention of re-building. The war intervened and, in 1939-40, the two chassis were sold to A. Barlow, a builder of miniature locomotives at Southport. The boiler, which was in good condition, was stored at Murthwaite but, because of its pattern and deep fire-box, was of no further use and is now dumped.

Dimensions will be found on p 130.

THE SECOND RIVER MITE

This 2–8–2, which returns to the Greenly concept of overscale models, actually belongs to the Preservation Society which ordered it in July 1964 and hired it to the Company on completion in December 1966. It is a straightforward 2–8–2 tender engine with outside cylinders and Walschaerts valve gear, similar in many respects to *River Esk*; indeed the chassis is basically the old Poultney tender one from *Esk* but the new locomotive incorporates a number of improvements. The main ones are equalised springing on the driving wheels, leaf springs being fitted in 1977; a much heavier pony truck with better springing; improved trailing wheel arrangement on the Cartozzi principle; generally more robust and simple fittings; a brake designed from the beginning for this locomotive. As can be seen from photographs, *River Mite* has a distinctive appearance of her own and is of very neat outline. It was built by Clarkson of York with a boiler by Gower's of Bedford and, after extended trials during the winter and spring of 1967, went into service for the 1967 season. Livery has varied in shade but has always been an approximation to Furness red with appropriate lining. A major overhaul and new firebox were provided in 1986-7.

No 10 Northern Rock. Even with the new *River Mite,* the railway was still short of motive power in the peak season and it was decided to design and build a new locomotive at Ravenglass. It was intended from the start to be constructed on maximum loading gauge principles, originally being envisaged as an 0–8–2 of vaguely colonial outline. The trials of the RH & D Pacific *Northern Chief* in 1971, when it worked at Ravenglass for a period, caused the railway to modify its ideas somewhat and the final design emerged as a neat 2–6–2 tender engine of typically British outline and with laminated springing instead of the rubber blocks initially envisaged. Apart from the boiler, the cylinder and wheel castings and various minor parts, the locomotive was built entirely in Ravenglass Works, being put into service during the Centenary year of 1976. It has proved a strong and valuable member of the stud. It is fitted with the standard boiler and has always been operated in a pleasant muscat green livery. In many ways the most aesthetically pleasing of the line's locomotives—at least to one imbued with Heywood ideals—the design has created a considerable amount of interest and may well be replicated for other railways.

No 11 Bonnie Dundee. This machine originated as a 2 ft gauge 0–4-0WT at Dundee Gas Works and was built by Kerr Stuart in 1900. In the 1960s it was acquired for preservation by Ian Fraser who gave it to the railway in 1976. Considerable thought was given as to how it could best be adapted and in 1981-2 it was transformed at Ravenglass into an 0–4–2 side tank engine with a sit-in cab and integral bunkers; the rear half of the overall cab is detachable for use in fine weather. It is capable reliably of pulling six loaded bogie coaches and is used

Footnote: It should be noted that, with the advent of airbrakes, all steam locomotives have been fitted with the necessary Duplex air pumps which can often be heard chuntering away while the locomotive is stationary.

Dimension	*Units*	*Sans Pareil*	*Colossus*	*Sir Aubrey Brocklebank*	*River Esk (as built)*	*River Irt*	*River Mite (1)*	*River Mite (2)*
Length with tender	ft in	9 0*	10 10¼*	10 10¾*	25 1¼	24 2	22 4	22 6
Width overall	ft in	2 5¼	2 5¼	2 5¼	3 2	3 10½	3 2?	3 1
Height to chimney/cab	ft in	3 7⅝	3 7¼	3 10¼	4 6⅝	4 7	5 2	4 8
Wheelbase (total)	ft in	7 0¾*	8 5⅜*	8 5⅜*	20 5¼	18 6	20 8	20 4½
„ (coupled)	ft in	1 9¾	3 6½	3 6½	5 0	6 0	3/6½+3/6½	5 0
Wheel dia (coupled)	in	20	20	20	17½	17½	20	17½
„ „ (bogie)	in	9⅜	9⅜	9⅜	—	—	9⅜	—
„ „ (truck)	in	10¼	10¼	10¼	12	10¼	—	11½
Wt with tender	t cwt	2 5	2 18	c 3t	6 18	6 5	N/K	c 6 18
Working pressure	psi	120	120	150	180	165	180	165
Heating surface	sq in	11,000	13,080	12,034	19,348	13,680	N/K	19,348
Cylinders dia	in	4⅛	4⅛	4⅛	5⅞	5⅝	(4) 4⅛	6
„ (stroke)	in	6¾	6¾	6¾	8½	8	(4) 6¾	8½
Valve gear		all inside Stephenson gear			Lentz poppet valve	Heywood	W'schaerts	W'schaerts

* Locomotive dimensions only

frequently in high season for extras and reliefs. Livery is North British Bronze Green.

Synolda. Though not in working stock, Ravenglass has once more acquired a Basset Lowke Class 30 Atlantic of the Sans Pareil type. *Synolda*, originally built for Sir Robert Walker's Sand Hutton Railway in Yorkshire, had a varied subsequent life but was eventually rescued from dereliction at Belle Vue Zoo, Manchester, in 1978. By the kindness of Trust House Forte, who donated her to the Eskdale Trust, and British Nuclear Fuels, whose apprentices rebuilt her, she is once more workable. She resides in the museum but occasionally has outings up the line and is kept in NGR-blue livery.

CHAPTER 11

Petrol and Diesel Tractors

THE KERR STUART

Standard gauge Kerr Stuart 0–6–0 diesel locomotive. This machine was obtained in December 1929 to work the standard gauge branch to Murthwaite, and its acquisition made the R & E a pioneer in the use of diesel traction. It was the first standard gauge diesel locomotive to be built by Kerr Stuart Limited and one of the first in Britain, being one of only two built to a 'standard' design of its maker. This was the biggest design in a series of three: 30, 60 and 90 hp respectively. It had a six-cylinder 90 hp McLaren Benz airless injection engine driving through a normal mechanical gearbox and final chain drive, all wheels being coupled by roller chains. Maker's number was 4421 and the livery was green, lined in yellow.

The first run was made on 6 December 1929, and after entering service, the locomotive worked most of the traffic right up to the end of stone traffic in 1953. When it was off for overhaul, a narrow-gauge Fordson was used to chain-haul standard gauge wagons to and from Murthwaite, but the Kerr Stuart appears to have been very reliable. It remained in store until 1955, and was then sold to the National Coal Board for use at Wingate Grange Colliery, Durham, where it still is. It is still in substantially original form except for having been re-engined with a Dorman diesel in 1960.

ICLS NOS 1 AND 2

15 in gauge Tractors

The Ford Model 'T' (first version). The first real i/c-engined tractor owned by the company was a most peculiar vehicle supplied by Francis Theakston Limited in 1922 or early 1923. It consisted basically of a Ford Model 'T' car chassis perched on a four-

Page 133: STONE TRAFFIC

[above] Partly-reconstructed crushing plant, showing one of the Fordsons. [centre] Murthwaite, showing old sector table and bins, also gravity-loaded wagons. [below] Tipping gear at Ravenglass, showing wagon being unloaded by gravity

Page 134: STANDARD GAUGE

[*above*] *'River Irt' pulls a motley train over the 'big points' onto mixed gauge track at Murthwaite* (*below*) *Murthwaite in standard gauge days with the Kerr Stuart diesel shunting*

wheel underframe, and has always aroused amusement among enthusiasts as to why this odd arrangement was adopted.

The reason appears to be that it was a standard ex-WD Light Railways Crewe Tractor. In 1916 and 1917, 132 of these had been built by the LNWR's Crewe Works for use on lightly-laid military tramways in France, and Mr Theakston had at the time been in charge of orders at the War Office. He probably remembered the design as being suitable for light lines and either constructed one or bought it secondhand. The latter is more likely, two examples in mint condition being advertised at about this period for sale by the War Surplus Disposals Board.

The original design had been intended as a road-rail convertible vehicle. It consisted of a steel-plate underframe with a 4 ft 5 in wheelbase, on which was mounted a complete Ford chassis. Drive was by inclined chain and sprocket from the normal Ford rear axle to the rear rail axle, rail axles being coupled by chain and sprocket and equipped with bandbrakes to guard against failure of the relatively-flimsy Ford rear axle. It was assumed that the car transmission reached maximum efficiency at about 25 mph and wheel diameters and ratios were therefore adjusted to give a rail speed of about 12 mph. There was no provision for fast reverse, but the machine had a built-in turning plate which could be lowered, thus lifting the car bodily off the rails and enabling it to be swung round to face the opposite direction.

At Ravenglass the machine was permanently fixed to its rail chassis, but the turning plate was retained. It was not liked, being considered a somewhat chancy operation, and the car was usually taken on to the nearest turntable unless sufficient men were available to deal with any upset. Turning was needed as the car had only one low reverse speed and this could not be used for long without serious overheating.

The car proved very useful for light mail trains and for staff work. The driver was very exposed to the elements and, for the winter of 1923-4, a peculiar hut-like cab was built over his seat. This made the appearance even more bizarre but did give him a modicum of comfort.

The car met its end on an evening trip to Dalegarth in Autumn 1925. Just opposite the CHA guest house one of the magnets on the flywheel worked loose and the whole of the dynamo disintegrated, bursting through the top half of the gearbox and spreading havoc and hot oil all round the cab. Luckily the driver escaped with only a few burns, but the car was finished.

ICL No 1. The Ford had proved so useful that it was decided to replace it as soon as possible. Its successor is always considered at Ravenglass as being in the nature of a rebuild, although only the old frame and parts of the epicyclic gearbox were used.

As a start, Ted Wright had built a channel-steel chassis, having the old frame converted to a rigid bogie at the rear, and a new swivelling bogie at the front. Drive was by the old Ford differential assembled on the front axle of the rigid bogie, the axles being coupled by chain and sprockets.

There was some delay in obtaining a new Model 'T' engine and, as a stopgap, Ted Wright fitted the chassis with a 9 hp Douglas engine from an ex-WD generating set. This, which had to be installed on a platform below the frame to maintain the correct centres for the Ford engine (the chassis arrangements being designed for this) was too light for the job but did useful work. The tractor was photographed as a bare chassis with this engine at Fell Dales Show 1926, thus unwittingly causing confusion for future historians, and was then fitted with a teak body resembling one of the old London Underground Camelback locomotives. This version can be recognised by the absence of headlamp portholes and, in some photographs, by the engine platform. Bits of the original gearbox, incidentally, were assembled with some spare parts to form a new one.

This version had a short life, the new Ford engine soon being fitted, together with headlamps and in this guise the tractor gave good service until, on 2 October 1928, it collided with ICL No 2 near Muncaster Mill. The Ford's body was reduced to matchwood, but the engine and chassis were not seriously damaged and it was decided to rebuild the machine as a matter of urgency.

Work began on 12 October and by the 26th of that month, the new body was complete! It was oblong in shape with long 'bonnets' and a low centre-cab which was said to be 'reminiscent of the NER electrics'. In this form, ICL No 1, rather oddly bearing a plate labelled ICL No 1 1927, which would appear to have no significance as a date at all, ran for the rest of her career as a motive power unit. Her disadvantages—lack of adhesion, the increasing problem of spares, and the fact that she had to be push-started—led to her seeing very little use once the Fordsons arrived and she was withdrawn early in the war when petrol became difficult to get. Nevertheless she remained officially on strength as a motive power unit until 1962, and visitors were always assured that she was serviceable and could be used in case of need!

By 1962, the motive power situation was quite good and everyone was tired of moving the 'Model T' from one place to another. She was therefore converted to a tool van, the engine being taken out and four seats fitted in the cab. As such she ran with the covered coaches for the 1962 season and was then relegated to staff use, doors being fitted for winter working. At present, she is kept at Dalegarth as the regular trailer for 'Billy's tractor', being used in winter as a mess and tool van for the permanent way staff. Dimensions will be found on p 141.

ICL No 2. More often known as 'the Lanchester', ICL No 2 was one of Ted Wright's improvisations, resulting from an urgent need for motive power which became obvious late in 1926. At that time the Heywood 0–6–0T *Ella* was needing a complete rebuild and Wright decided to convert her to a petrol locomotive instead.

Work began on 10 January 1927. *Ella*'s frames and wheels were used as a basis, the frames being extended 2 ft at each end to take an extra pair of wheels. The arrangement was thus 2–6–2, with limited lateral play on the end axles. On this foundation was mounted a complete Lanchester Model 38 touring car chassis, sawn off at the dash, but retaining its six-cylinder engine and the gearbox. A Parson's Marine direct reverse gear was fitted to this box to permit equal speeds in each direction, and a universal joint fed power thence to the original Lanchester worm drive. A solid shaft and final chain drive replaced the old differential, and all driving wheels were coupled with rods. Finally, a home-built body was built of tongue-and-groove teak boards and the locomotive was put in service in the spring of 1927.

ICL No 2 proved to be an excellent investment, being reasonably fast and yet capable of hauling heavy loads; in fact there is a photograph, obviously posed, to show she could haul as much as *Green Goddess* had done on trial! On 2 October 1928, she collided head-on with ICL No 1, reducing the latter's body to matchwood and distorting her own none-too-strong frame. The frame was more or less straightened but was never quite the same afterwards. She had a punishing time during the hard winter that followed and, in the spring of 1929, pushed a big-end through the crank case. It proved almost impossible to obtain spare parts, the Lanchester Model 38 having been obsolescent even when she was built, and, with the advent of the standard gauge, she was quietly retired. Tom Jones' diary mentions work being done on her in January 1930, but she was never returned to service and was scrapped by instalments. Her frames were still lying at Murthwaite

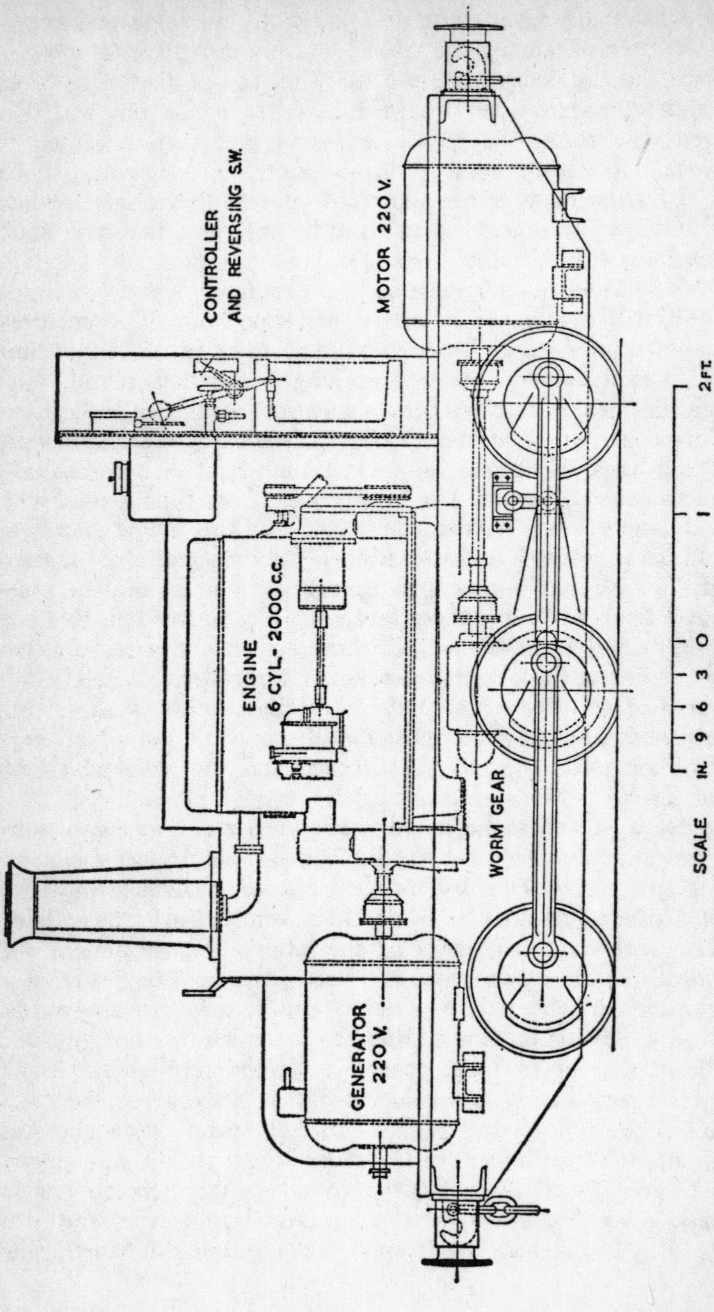

(9) *P/E project for* Ella *conversion*

when the new company took over in 1960! Livery during her short life was varnished teak.

THE FORDSONS

The Muir-Hill Fordson tractors. Three of these four-wheel petrol tractors were ordered late in 1927 for use between Quarry and Murthwaite. They were built by Muir-Hill Service Equipment Limited of Trafford Park near Manchester, a company very well known for its road dumper trucks, and were powered by Fordson 20 hp tractor engines driving through special Muir-Hill gearboxes giving two speeds in each direction. Final drive was to one axle by roller chain and sprockets, the axles being coupled by chains and running in roller-bearing boxes. The tractors were cabless, but a light roof supported on pillars was supplied as an additional attachment, at least one tractor being equipped with this. Their normal load was sixteen loaded wagons.

These tractors have caused some confusion. From company records, one, bearing no manufacturer's number, was delivered in January 1928 but developed a gearbox fault which may have delayed delivery of the others. The original box had trunnions cast integrally and fitting into two bearings on the chassis; these tended to break in service conditions, possibly because the arrangement was too rigid to absorb shocks, and they had to be replaced by steel bars fixed across the gearbox top.

As a result, the other two were delivered in 1929, NG 39 being unloaded on 15 March, and NG 41 on 2 April. They, too, received the gearbox modification and all then gave very satisfactory service.

During the early 1930s, the need for a petrol passenger tractor to replace ICL No 2 became obvious and about 1933 NG 39 was rebuilt as an 0–4–4PP with a trailing bogie on frame extensions and a body vaguely resembling a steam locomotive of the side tank variety. It was used for stone traffic during the war but returned to passenger work afterwards and proved invaluable—indeed it is doubtful if the service could have been run without the unit. By the mid-1970s, however, spares were getting almost impossible to obtain and in 1975 it was rebuilt with a Perkins 6-cylinder diesel of 45 hp, necessitating a rather ugly extension to the bonnet. Even this had to be considered in the light of a temporary refurbishment and in 1984-5 it was taken into Ravenglass Works and comprehensively rebuilt to diesel outline with a fully enclosed cab and a new engine. Ceremonially named *Perkins* in May 1985, it has been painted yellow and is used mainly for shunting and PW work. It has air brake equipment, however, and can haul passenger trains if required.

The other two tractors continued in use until 1953 but were then cannibalised to provide one serviceable unit, named *Quarryman*. This was fitted with a backless cab (it might be better described as a shelter!) and for many years lived at Dalegarth as reserve and general dogsbody. Following the centenary it was withdrawn from regular use and restored to its original cabless state with Fordson radiator. It is nominally allocated to the museum but is still used from time to time.

Royal Anchor. This was an experimental B-B diesel hydraulic locomotive built in 1956 by the late Charles Lane of the Royal Anchor Hotel, Liphook, Hants, in collaboration with a Mr J. R. Green. It was tried on the R H & D R and then stored until 1961 when the R & E R tried it and bought it from Mr Lane's executors. Powered by a Ford 4D diesel engine it could haul four coaches over the R & E R, though the experimental transmission was not very efficient. However it performed sterling work at a time when any item of motive power was welcome and was not pensioned off until 1978 when the remains were sold to Steamtown Carnforth. On the R & E R it was painted first two-tone grey with red trim and then royal blue.

Shelagh of Eskdale. In late 1967, the existing parts for Tom Jones's projected 4–6–4 diesel were sent off to Severn Lamb Ltd and used to build a new locomotive; it was named after a legendary local Viking heroine. At the time the railway was very interested in diesel-hydraulic drive and the locomotive accordingly had a Ford 4D diesel driving its coupled axles through standard Linde hydraulic units. In appearance she was a neat and pleasing design with full width cab each end of the body and a totally enclosed engine section accessed by side panels. There were the usual pioneering teething troubles; indeed the original drive was never troublefree but in 1979 she was re-engined with a Perkins 6-cylinder, 112 hp diesel and given upgraded hydraulic units. At the same time the original blue livery was replaced by two-tone green. She has recently spent much time away, working at Romney for a year to prove the diesel concept and then providing reserve power for the 1984 Liverpool Garden Festival. She also worked, briefly, at Britannia Theme Park at Derby in the 1985 season.

Silver Jubilee. The railway had for some years felt a need for a light and economical train. In 1976, therefore, new coach bodies were used to construct a two-car diesel hydraulic set, with a Ford 4D engine working through a second-hand Linde transmission, ex *Shelagh of Eskdale*... During winter 1976-7 the set was properly fitted out,

INTERNAL COMBUSTION-ENGINE TRACTORS

Dimension	*Units*	*Crewe Tractor*	*ICL No 1 (orig)*	*ICL No 1 (final)*	*ICL No 2*	*Fordson 4-wheel*	*Fordson 0–4–4*	*Royal Anchor*
Wheel arr	—	4 wheel	4 w+bogie	4 w+bogie	2–6–2	4-wheel	0–4–4	B-B
Length over buffer beams	ft in	11 0	15 0	15 0	10 8	9 6	13 6	14 7
Width overall	ft in	5 3⅜	3 5	3 5	3' 10	3 7	3 3	3 4
Height over rail	ft in	4 6	N/K	5 4	N/K	7 7	5 11	5 3
Wheelbase—total	ft in	4 5	N/K	12 10	6 6	3 0	8 7	12 0
„ —rigid	ft in	4 5	4 5	4 5	4 6*	3 0	3 0	2 1½
Wheel dia —driving	ft in	1 6	1 6	1 6	1 1½	1 8	1 8	9⅞
—idler	ft in	—	1 0	1 0	1 0	—	10	—
Motor—hp		20	20	20	38	20	20	60
—cyls	No	4	4	4	6	4	4	4
Fuel		petrol	petrol	petrol	petrol	TVO	TVO	Diesel

* with radial action on centre drivers

being styled with neat, wedge-shaped ends to motor and driving trailer. In honour of the Queen's silver jubilee it was named *Silver Jubilee* and painted silver with blue trim. A centre coach was added to increase capacity and the set ran thus until 1979, doing a fair amount of work in spite of various teething troubles. It was tinkered with over succeeding years and then completely rebuilt as a four-car set with two powercars for the 1984 Liverpool festival where it ran a branch shuttle. During the 5½ months it was there it made 7,161 return journeys and carried 572,880 passengers according to railway statistics. For this it was painted in BR intercity style which it still retains. Dimensions are similar to those of the bogie closed coaches though the more elegant end profile increases powercar length by about 12 inches.

Lady Wakefield. The increasing age of Perkins led the railway to embark on construction of a further new diesel locomotive in 1978-9. Work started at Ravenglass in mid 1979 and the result is a B-B diesel mechanical machine capable of pulling a full train. It is a handsome design powered by a Perkins 112 hp 6-cylinder diesel and driving one axle of each bogie through a British Twin Disc torque converter and a powershift transmission. Final drive is from a chain-driven transfer box to cardan shafts acting on the inner axle of each bogie via a worm and wheel gear train; bogie axles are coupled by chains. Externally the locomotive has a two-seat cab at one end with the power unit under a long, louvred hood. It entered service in mid 1980 and, apart from a short visit to Romney has been in use ever since. Livery is maroon with cream trim.

Miscellaneous Locomotives. The railway acquired, in 1981, a four wheeled Greenwood and Batley battery electric locomotive. It is regarded more as a works shunter than a serious machine (though it has worked through to Dalegarth) and, when operative, is used mainly around Ravenglass. In 1985-6 a group of Preservation Society members officially styling themselves the Murthwaite Locomotive Group acquired a Lister 4WD locomotive which they have named *Cyril* and restored for permanent way use.

SCOOTERS

The R & ER produced a number of 'one-off' scooters at various times in the 1920s, mainly for use on PW and winter mail duty. The first was powered by a device known as the Wall Autowheel, a forerunner of present day moped engines, and was a simple four-wheeled trolley carrying a wicker basket. It died spectacularly in head-on collision with *Sans Pareil* in 1921 or 1922 but the idea had been proved sound. It was soon replaced by another four-wheeled trolley powered by a 2½ hp Economic engine and boasting a seatbox for the driver. This saw quite frequent use on winter trains and even acquired a front shield reminiscent of present-day motor scooters. It appears to have been disused by 1925, when the new regime took over.

Only one further genuine scooter was constructed by the Gillon regime but some confusion has been caused because the chassis of ICL No 1, when fitted with a Douglas 9 hp engine, was taken out on trial and photographed thus by Mary Fair. The genuine one was *The Scott*, built during April and May 1927 to keep 'the office' in contact with Quarry and Crushing Plant. *The Scott* was so called because it comprised a frame, made from an old bogie, fitted with a Scott Squirrel twin-cylinder water-cooled two-stroke engine, the whole being covered by a crude body. Capable of up to about 50 mph,, it was very popular among the staff who appeared unworried by the fact that it had no brakes. After a telephone line was installed between Ravenglass and Murthwaite in 1930, it fell out of use and was scrapped.

One more scooter was fabricated in 1971 at Ravenglass for occasional use by track gangs. It comprised a four-wheeled frame originally fitted with a Villiers 197 cc two-stroke engine and a small windscreen. Later fitted with a 125 cc BSA four-stroke, it was, in the tradition of its predecessor, fast and not easy to stop but has survived to reach the museum.

CHAPTER 12

15 in Gauge Rolling-Stock

COACHES

Bassett-Lowke four-wheelers. The original vehicles supplied in 1915 comprised a set of Bassett-Lowke's standard four-wheel open cars as produced for many miniature railways. These were straightforward vehicles seating eight passengers transversely in two compartments and can best be described by quoting the specification from the Bassett-Lowke catalogue of Garden Railways Equipment.

> The Bodies are made up from best well-seasoned Burmese teak with a good figure and grain. The sides are framed up in heavy stuff and panelled up in best style with teak matching. Cast iron steps are fitted to each entrance. The Bodies are fixed to the Underframes with iron knees and can be easily removed for transport and repairs. The Underframes are constructed of the best English oak on the most approved lines. They are stiffened with steel longitudinal and cross stays and steel headstock bolts with forged palm pieces.

The catalogue then describes in detail the central 'buckeye' combined buffer-couplings which were pivoted from the underframe to avoid straining the headstocks, and mentions the sprung, oil-lubricated axleboxes and the vacuum brakes before concluding:

> The coaches are finished in the best quality out-door varnish and lined with gold and blue lines. Underframes are painted best black enamel over the best lead paint. All iron work is black and the floor inside best grey paint... They can be lettered to order in gold shaded letters or, if preferred, with solid brass letters.

The Ravenglass coaches, or at least the original set, were in fact lettered 'Eskdale Express' in brass on the body centre panels and some also had the optional extras advertised by Bassett-Lowke. These were teak-framed glass windscreens—normally one per coach, fitted at one end—and metal-framed gaily-striped awnings more suitable to a garden railway than to the R & E. Indeed they obviously proved useless, for several coaches were quickly fitted with what appear from photographs to be standard touring car hoods, complete with back window! These could be dismantled when required. It should be noted here that windscreen-fitted coaches were normally run in sets of two with a screen at each end and the slip coaches for Irton Road usually consisted of a set with more vehicles added if required. Vacuum brakes were fitted but later dismantled.

The exact number of the coaches is in doubt but was eventually either eleven or twelve. The originals, seven in number, came from Oslo with the engine. The rest were obtained later either from Staughton Manor or, more likely, from the Sand Hutton Railway which had four and from which a saloon coach did reach the R & E. These may have been the coaches modified to have doors to each compartment, three or possibly four vehicles having this feature for some time in the early twenties.

Most of the Bassett-Lowke coaches continued in use until the 1930s although two were converted, perhaps temporarily, to flat wagons about 1923; in this guise they conveyed new coach bodies to Irton Road. They were gradually replaced from 1924 onward by six somewhat similar four-wheelers and by new bogie stock. The last time they ran as a train was in 1934 and from then on they were kept in reserve in a steadily-deteriorating condition. A few survived the 1939-45 war in running order, but now (1967) only one body is left, in bad condition.

At least one coach was modified in the early days of the Mitchell régime for use on winter trains. The sides were covered with vertical matchboarding to a height of about 5 ft and a flat roof was fitted; this gave a reasonably weatherproof vehicle which could yet be towed by the first light scooters.

Dimensions	*Bassett-Lowke* 4-*w*	*Locally-built* 4-*w*
Length over headstocks	8 ft 2 in	9 ft 5 in
Width over body	3 ft 2 in	3 ft 4 in
Height from rail	—	5 ft 4 in (with roof)
Wheelbase	5 ft 8 in	6 ft 4 in
Wheel dia on tread	10½ in	12 in

Locally-built four-wheel coaches. These six coaches were built in 1922-3, possibly by railway staff, for Henry Greenly records that 'they are now building at Ravenglass, Mr Geo Dale being in charge of the work'. Recollections locally are that the bodies were built by Dawson of Barrow and merely assembled into their running gear at Irton Road during the autumn of 1923. In support of this all photographs of the work show the bodies complete and resting on flat wagons which have apparently brought them there.

They were generally similar to the Bassett-Lowke vehicles, being two-compartment eight-seaters with teak-panelled bodies, but were more angular in appearance and had oak underframes. End screens were not fitted but they did have vacuum brakes. They were all still in regular service when the society took over in 1960.

The new company rebuilt all six as covered vehicles to form a wet-weather train behind *Royal Anchor*. The conversion, carried out in 1962, entailed fitting solid end-bulkheads and a well-cambered roof, and re-painting in maroon. Two coaches were fitted for train headboards, a relic of their first season when they formed '*The Rambler*', the only named train to run on the railway. They were a useful set, though not much liked by steam engine drivers as their coupling springs were weak and could lead to drag in starting a heavy train. They are now withdrawn and converted into stores vans and service vehicles; one is preserved for a possible future museum. Dimensions will be found on p 145.

Heywood-type bogie stock—Introduction. The position regarding Heywood stock is very confusing and has recently been further complicated by evidence which indicates that published references are inaccurate. The following notes are based on all available evidence, including the assumption that all surviving Duffield Bank stock was acquired, and on photographic evidence that, after 1925 at least, there were seven Heywood-type closed coaches including the dining and sleeping cars—and the fact that it was necessary to rebuild the latter after a prolonged period of disuse at Irton Road would indicate that no other vehicles were available.

Until now it has been assumed that, as early writers recorded four open and four closed coaches at Ravenglass as well as the dining and sleeping cars, this number came from Duffield Bank. Recently, two items have come to light which throw doubt on this assumption. One is the sale catalogue for the Duffield Bank auction which shows only four open coaches and the sleeping car, plus one closed coach nearing completion—the latter was almost certainly a replacement for a closed coach sent to Ravenglass the previous year.

The other item is an undated and incomplete NGR blueprint of a Heywood-pattern closed coach with notes indicating that the company had already built one or more of these vehicles, together with the comment that 'these coaches are now built 2 in higher from rail level to bottom of solebar and from 3 to 4 in higher from solebar to top runner ie height of doors'. Certainly one of the five closed coaches running on the line in the late 20s did differ from the rest in these respects; while, of the remaining four, only one can definitely be identified as a Duffield Bank vehicle. The other three differ in minor details, including lighter scantlings and the provision of solid, planked end-screens to the balconies in place of the conventional Heywood steel bar. There are also photographs showing either new construction or at least drastic rebuilding of Heywood-type stock about 1922-3 at Irton Road, and it must be noted that both the dining and sleeping cars were extensively rebuilt during the 20s to provide extra accommodation.

It therefore seems certain that NGR Limited built at least three Heywood-type closed coaches and probably completed the partly-built one from Duffield Bank. The company had a very good ex-seaman carpenter at the time who was quite capable of doing the job, and the writer has always wondered why Heywood should ever have had more than one closed coach at Duffield. After all, open vehicles were much more suitable for the 'fête days' when heavy traffic was carried and he did state that the one closed coach and van existing at the time he wrote his book had been built simply to show that it was feasible on such a small gauge.

(*a*) *'Standard' closed coaches.* As far as is known, four of these vehicles were used at Ravenglass. They were sixteen-seater bogie coaches with room for twelve passengers seated transversely in three compartments and two more on outside balconies at each end. This rather curious arrangement was to achieve a low centre of gravity, the compartment floors being fixed to the bottom of the coach solebars to form a well. The solebars themselves were of 9 in x 3 in pitch-pine baulks joined by four wooden cross-members, and construction was of wood throughout. The raised end-balconies were on top of the frames with bogie pivots under each outward-facing end seat and the bogies were crude wooden affairs with a wheelbase of only 18 in.

These coaches received hard use and, despite continual patching and re-building, were in very bad condition by the early 1930s, during which they were withdrawn one by one. Exact dates are not known, but none survived the 1939-45 war.

These coaches can be differentiated in photographs by slight variations in height and by differing end-screens to the balconies. Most of the doors were removed in the late 1920s as they tended to foul Dalegarth platform when the three-track layout was in use and thus became easily damaged.

(*b*) *Odd closed coach.* There was a fifth Heywood-type coach of normal pattern but differing considerably from the others in bodywork detail and in the shape of the solebars, which had flush tops. The vehicle was higher than the others, with a roof camber approximating that of the sleeping car, and had a different window arrangement—there are just two big windows between each door, not the normal two small ones with a panel in between—and a single circular porthole was inserted in each end bulkhead.

(*c*) *Heywood open coaches.* All four of the open bogie coaches from Duffield came to Ravenglass. These were similar in appearance and dimensions to the closed vehicles but were open above the waist and had doorless entrances to the 'compartments'. They were piped but not fitted with brakes, the piping running along the outside of one side frame. Seats originally had leather cushions.

These coaches were used extensively both for passenger traffic and for the goods traffic in bagged wool which flourished sporadically in the early 1920s. Gillon in 1931 records them as being all worn-out and unsafe for traffic and they were apparently withdrawn about that time, probably being replaced by the new open coaches then building (see p 155).

(*d*) *The dining car.* In its original form, the dining car was laid out as shown in Fig 10, with seats and tables for eight people, and a small kitchen which included that invaluable Victorian item, a Rippingill Oil Stove—a contraption often found in the cramped galleys of contemporary small yachts but rarely on a railway! It was the only Heywood coach without side doors although droplights were provided in the normal door positions. Entrance was by end doors opening from the normal Heywood pattern of end balcony and thence down into the coach 'well'. At Ravenglass, this method of entry was continued but the doors themselves were soon removed.

Modification of this coach for the R & E was relatively easy, consisting simply of removing the small kitchen and the partition between that and the 'dining saloon' and in fitting four more seats on the original pattern. This appears to have been done fairly soon after arrival and the coach lasted longer than most of the other Heywood vehicles. It was in any case probably in better

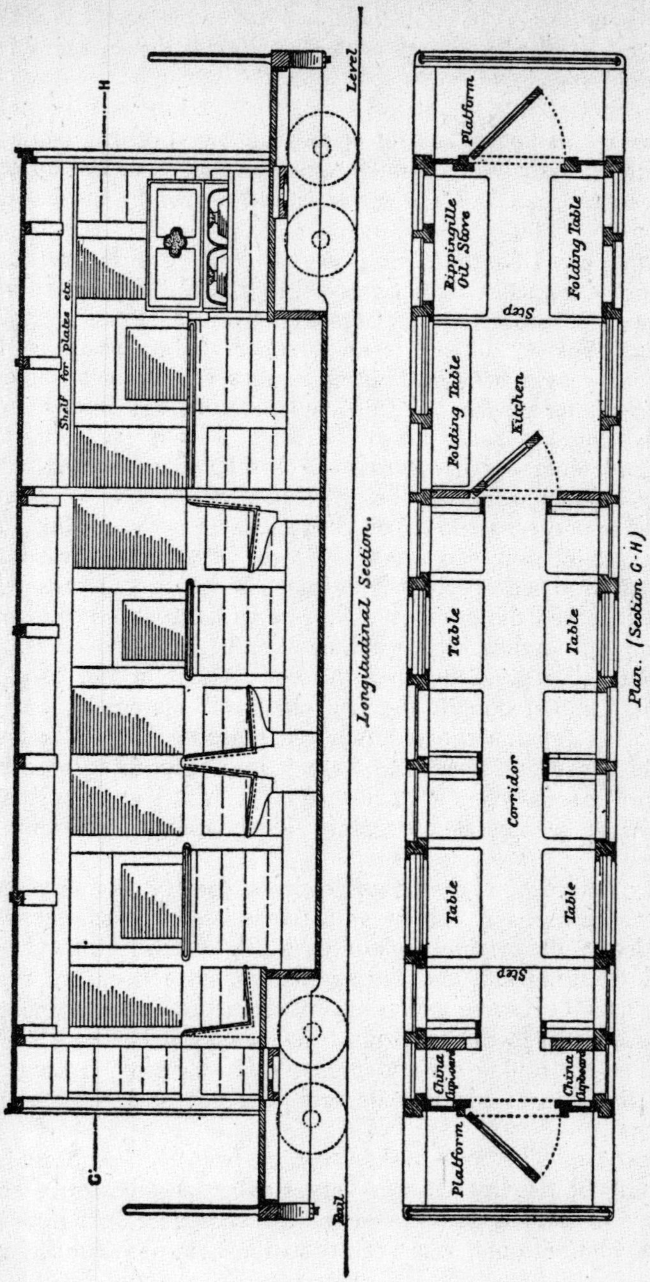

(10) Heywood dining car

structural condition as it would not have had much use at Duffield and the lack of door openings in the body sides would make for a more rigid structure.

The coach was in use on staff trains up to about 1939. It was then taken off its bogies and for some years stood on the bank at Murthwaite as a shelter and messroom. The body was not broken up until about 1948 and the frame is still buried in the undergrowth.

The sleeping car. Like the dining car, this bogie vehicle was built more to prove a theory than for practical use, although some use was made of it as overflow accommodation during times of stress at Duffield Bank. It differed from all other Heywood coaches in having a full-length body without end balconies, this being necessary to accommodate the two full-length double-deck bunks sited diagonally opposite each other as shown in Fig 11. Entrance was by single doors in the centre of each side, with flanking windows, the bodyside otherwise being wood-panelled save for single droplights opposite each pair of berths. As with the dining car, maximum height from rail was 6 ft which, with an outside width of only 3 ft 6 in, left sleepers little room in which to manoeuvre although they had the use of a folding wash basin and a 'dressing table'—actually a shelf with a mirror over it.

The Mitchell régime acquired this car as part of the bargain when NGR Limited bought the Duffield Bank equipment, but it was obviously not thought worthwhile to perform the considerable amount of conversion needed to make it into an ordinary passenger coach. For some years it languished off its bogies at Irton Road, being used as a store and sleeping accommodation for summer workers.

In 1925, the new régime needed closed coaches urgently and the car was completely rebuilt as a twelve-seater. The task was made easier by the original style of panelling which facilitated the fitting of windows and the cutting of two extra doors on each side. Ordinary transverse seats were fitted, in three compartments, and the coach ran in this form until the closed coaches were withdrawn. Like the dining car and probably for the same reasons, it survived the war at Murthwaite and was not broken up until about 1951.

Bogie brake van. The bogie brake van came from Duffield Bank for the opening of the line. It was very similar in appearance and dimensions to the standard closed coaches except for its length of 15 ft, with end balconies and a centre van portion with two sliding

Page 151: MODERN STOCK

[*above*] *'River Esk' draws into No 1 Platform at Ravenglass while 'Silver Jubilee' waits in the middle road.* [*centre*] *'Northern Rock' crosses over from the main line to run into Platform 1 while 'River Irt' awaits a road to the Loco Shed.* [*below*] *'Lady Wakefield' basks in the sunshine outside the Diesel Shed, sporting her new livery*

Page 152: MORE MODERN STOCK

[*above*] *'River Mite' pulls away out o Ravenglass over the road bridge.* [*centre 'River Irt's' new outline is strikingly differen Compare with photo on page 98.* [*below 'Bonnie Dundee' when 'new' ready to leav Platform 3. The coach is 'Silver Jubilee's centre saloon*

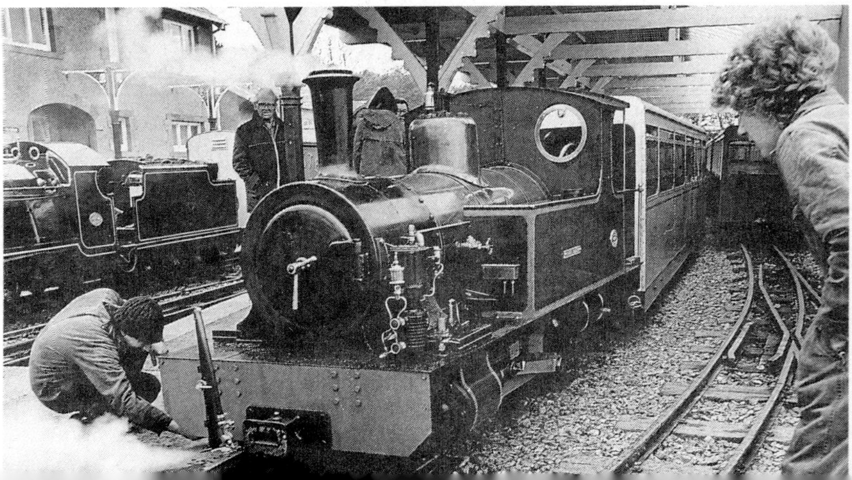

doors on each side. Seats were provided on the balconies for four people.

The van was intended for passengers' luggage, but proved too heavy to be of much use, a light wagon being substituted to ease the over-strained motive power. The van body was thereupon borrowed by Bob Hardie, who took it off to Irton Road and kept chickens in it. After he left, in 1925, it was taken to Beckfoot Quarry where it acted as a shelter for the quarrymen until it was demolished by a runaway wagon in 1940.

The 'Glass Coach'. This vehicle was something of an oddity. It was originally built for Sir Robert Walker's 15 in gauge Sand Hutton Railway, in 1913-4. It came from that line in the early 1920s, probably in 1922, when conversion of the SHR to 18 in gauge was taking place. It was a very lightly-built bogie saloon with eight large windows along each side, and enclosed end vestibules. It was very popular at Ravenglass for winter and special workings because it was a good runner and light enough to be pulled easily by the various scooters. Its very light construction meant that it wore out very quickly and it was withdrawn about 1927. Certainly by the summer of 1928 it was in use as a summerhouse in a garden just above Ravenglass turntable.

The main peculiarity of the coach at Ravenglass was its seating. Ken Hartley, in his book on the SHR, states that it was a ten-seater with centre gangway and sliding doors from the vestibules, but this was not so at Ravenglass. Photographs show three seat-backs extending clear across the coach. This arrangement must have led to some gymnastics by 'inside passengers' even if the backs could be removed, and would seem to be very complicated. It would also appear that the sliding doors, at diagonally opposite corners of the vehicle, were also removed, for photographs taken on winter trains in 1924-5 show tarpaulin aprons hung across the saloon doorways. The livery at Sand Hutton was varnished teak, but it is not certain if this continued to be so at Ravenglass. No dimensions are available.

Locally-built bogie open coaches. The railway has always been attracted to open coaches because of the beautiful scenery through which it passes. Eskdale in good weather can best be appreciated from such a vehicle and it is notable that, unless it is actually raining or blowing a gale, the open coaches are the first to fill up. The first set of six, though numbered 1/27—6/27, was actually built in late 1928, largely from teak ships' timbers acquired as part of a job lot via the Company's Cunard connections; they have proved so hardwearing that they were withdrawn from service only in 1986 and may yet be refurbished. 16-seaters, they set the standard for subsequent batches, differing from the Heywoods in having flush floors and four compartments in place of the latters' three compartments and outward-facing end seats. Their components were built mainly by Dawsons of Barrow and assembled by the railway carpenter but later batches, built largely from pitch-pine, were constructed entirely at Ravenglass. These comprised a batch of four in 1932 (1/32 to 4/32); four in 1933 (1/33 to 4/33); and two more, appropriately numbered, in each of 1934 and 1935. These twelve coaches had deeper centre portions to the side frames and four tie-bars a side instead of five. After withdrawal of the Heywood vehicles they, plus the teaks, constituted the railway's entire bogie stock until 1951, although one disappeared during the war.

From 1952 onwards, the '1930s' stock was steadily replaced by similar vehicles as it wore out, and nine additional coaches were built, some having hardboard panelling instead of planks. The heavy wastage was due mainly to the fact that, up to 1966, vehicles were stored mainly in the open but, equally, many components such as bogies, ironwork and seats were reutilised with new frames. At a 1967 stock check, some 26 sixteen seaters were in service; by 1977 all but the six teaks were withdrawn, their demise speeded by a 1969 derailment in the carriage shed and by the 1976 collision which showed that vehicles with drawgear on the bogies were not as safe as those with it affixed to the underframe. They have been replaced largely with a 20-seater design to the old Heywood seating pattern—ie four compartments and two outward facing end seats. Most have flush floors, a single 1966-vintage prototype with metal frame and dropped floor (1/66) not being perpetuated; subsequent vehicles have been built at Ravenglass on wood frames. The first were equipped with fittings from scrapped vehicles but latterly new, plywood panelled bodies with high-back seats have been fitted. Livery was green/black until 1979, then progressively maroon/black and, from 1986 for some new vehicles, varnished wood.

Jaywick coaches. These three coaches were bogie, two-compartment eight-passenger vehicles with upholstered seating and window curtains, their length of 17 ft 6 in allowing unlimited legroom for passengers. The underframes were steel and the ash-framed bodies were covered in plywood panelling and galvanised metal sheeting. The coaches were painted at Ravenglass in Furness blue-and-white with grey roofs. They were built by Caffyn of Eastbourne in 1936 for the Jaywick Miniature Railway near Clacton in Essex. On the closure of that line in 1939 they were stored and, after the war, went to a pleasure line in New Brighton. They were acquired by the R & E R at the end of 1965, being regauged and repaired in time for the 1966 season. Although heavy, they were popular and a supplementary fare was at first charged for travelling in them. They were all withdrawn and sold to Pen y Orsedd in 1978.

Closed saloon coaches. The Jaywicks showed the desirability of a train of closed vehicles and, following trials of an open prototype, two saloons were bought from Myers & Bowman of Distington. They were, and are, twenty seaters, built almost entirely of aluminium and with sliding doors on the south side only. They were designed at Ravenglass and have several interesting features, including louvre windows instead of droplights in the sides which have no doorways. To save height, the floor is dropped, Heywood fashion, between the frames and the seating arrangement is 2–4–4–4–4–2. This means that at one end there is no room for a sliding door and a hinged one was provided. To give passengers the best view, coaches are open inside above the seatbacks and have large windows. They also have single windows in each end.

The vehicles proved so successful that their number has been steadily increased though all later ones have been built by Edmund Crow of Cleator Moor. Successive batches have incorporated modifications found desirable in service, the most noticeable being the replacement of Louvre windows by large picture windows having full-length hopper ventilators; several are fitted with guards' compartments. Two of the later vehicles were adapted as powercars for *Silver Jubilee* (qv) and one bodyshell was specially constructed to run with that set for the 1984 Liverpool Garden Festival. It differs from others in the series in having a central entrance with folding doors, and perimeter seating to allow the carriage of wheelchairs.

Semi-open coaches. A compromise between visibility and comfort, these vehicles are built to the same dimensions and profile as closed coaches but are open above the waist and have wood-seated compartments with doorless entrances; they are very popular with passengers. As a result of Lord Wakefield's concern for the disabled, several of them are specially fitted so that they can, if required, carry wheelchair passengers; three sets of seats are removable and a side panel can be detached so that two wheelchairs can be loaded by means of ramps. An interesting innovation also is the fitting of some vehicles with blued translucent roofs—it does little to improve visibility but presumably brightens up Eskdale on a grey day!

WAGON STOCK

Heywood open wagons. The first wagons to run at Ravenglass were standard open wagons of Heywood manufacture from Duffield Bank. The exact number is uncertain but there seem to have been about a dozen and they were used both for general goods traffic (especially coal and ballast) and as temporary coaches at peak periods. For the latter purpose they were fitted with low-back seats installed at each end and these can be seen on page 88.

In accordance with Heywood's principles, the wagons were designed for a range of uses. They were basically flat trucks on which could be fitted either bolsters, for timber-carrying, (Page 57) or, more usually, sides and ends built as 'Box' units. The standard box was 6 ft x 3 ft inside and 1 ft 3 in high. It was located on the flat wagon by strong corner brackets. The height could be increased by adding detachable 'tops' and up to 2 tons could be carried by later versions. As with the coaches, springing was replaced by rubber blocks.

It appears likely that the wagons which came to Ravenglass comprised all the surviving stock for from photographic evidence they included not only the standard variety but also a few of Heywood's earlier version, which measured only 4 ft x 2 ft inside. Most passenger trains included at least one of these latter as a luggage truck and one is said to have been fitted with ridged roof for carrying the mails. This would agree with the fact that there was a similar vehicle at Duffield, used for storing PW equipment.

Heywood bogie wagon. The R & E also acquired from Duffield Bank an open three-ton capacity bogie wagon of Heywood design. It had a wooden body with single-unit drop sides about 1 ft 6 in high mounted on a frame similar to those of his open coaches; it appears on pages 57 and 87. It was out of use by 1925, being dumped off its bogies at Irton Road yard and, by 1927, was rotting away upside-down beside the siding there.

Granite wagons.

The exact position regarding granite wagons is unclear, various dates and manufacturers having been quoted, but the following appears most probable. For the opening of Beckfoot Quarry, F. Theakston Limited supplied the complete equipment consisting of eighteen wood-and-metal four-wheel wagons with drop doors for use between Quarry and Murthwaite; six two-ton tippler wagons for Murthwaite—Ravenglass traffic, and a tippler installation at

Ravenglass. The number of Theakston wagons was soon increased to sixty and, after 1925, a small number of similar wagons were bought from Wilkinson of Workington, probably about a dozen in all. The final 'strength' was sixty-four in service at any one time, sixteen at the quarry, sixteen at Murthwaite, and sixteen *en route*, with sixteen spare. Most were broken up on behalf of the Keswick Granite Company by the railway soon after 1960, but the company was allowed to keep six of each type, which are still in use for PW work. Some now run without their doors.

Theakston wagons. These were metal-bodied wagons with bottom-hinge flap doors and can be recognised in photographs by their high sides and curved bottoms to the ends. They could carry 26 cwt or 1.29 cu yd and were well-built, some having metal frames and some wood. All survivors are metal-framed.

Wilkinson wagons. These were similar, but with lower sides and straight ends. They had metal frames and bodies, carried 23 cwt (1.20 cu yd) and are said to have been made with low sides so that the quarrymen did not have to lift the stone so high.

Theakston tippler wagons. These were to carry the crushed stone from Murthwaite to Ravenglass and could take two tons. They were all-metal, but had very flimsy frames and narrow tyres, so were not very popular and soon relegated to spares. Their long, bath-shaped bodies proved useful later on as water tanks! Although none now survives intact, one body and frame lasted as the water tank at Ravenglass until 1963, while another is still *in situ* at the Fisherground watering point. Two others had their frames used to carry, respectively, fuel-oil tanks and the weed-killing wagon, the latter still being in use.

Dimensions	*Units*	*Theakston side-door*	*Wilkinson side-door*
Length over headstocks	ft in	6 6	6 7
Width overall	ft in	3 0	3 0
Height from rail	ft in	3 10	3 6
Wheelbase	ft in	3 4½	3 4½
Wheel dia	in	14	14

Bogie granite hopper wagons.

In February 1927 it was decided to do away with the tippling gear at Ravenglass and a modern all-steel bogie hopper wagon was designed by the railway staff to take its place. The wagon held six tons and had two bottom-discharge hoppers with baffle plates; the hoppers were discharged by a sliding grid in the floor operated by twin screw wheels. These were operated simultaneously by an external ratchet handle. Length over headstocks was about 21 ft; width 3 ft, and height over rail 3 ft 9 in.

Six of these wagons were constructed by the Yorkshire Engine Company during 1927 and the early part of 1928: their first trial runs were made in May 1928. They tended to run hot but, after modification of the axlebox arrangement, they proved excellent wagons. In spite of this they had a short life for, when the standard gauge was put in in 1929-30, they were sold to the Romney, Hythe & Dymchurch Railway as ballast wagons. The bogies were bought back in 1931 when RH & D replaced them with Gibbons bogies and the wheels and axleboxes were used for the construction of eight four-wheel wagons. Some parts were later incorporated in coaches of the 1933 batch. The wagons themselves continued in service with the RH & D until the war when some of them formed the basis of an armoured train. After the war the five survivors were all dismantled and the underframes used for the construction of coaches.

General-purpose four-wheel wagons.

Heywood-type wagons. In 1931-2 a set of eight wooden-side wagons were built at Ravenglass to the original Heywood design to replace Heywood wagons that had been withdrawn. They can be recognised in photographs by their natural wood finish and large black-metal corner plates. They were used until 1953 for chippings traffic from Murthwaite to the road chute at Ravenglass and then rotted away.

Other wagons built at Murthwaite. It was established practice during the Gillon régime to 'knock-up' wooden wagons as required from wood lying around at Murthwaite plant. 8 in x 6 in beams were simply sawn to length, tenoned into headstocks, fitted with flooring and running gear, and there was a wagon. Tom Jones reckons that over a hundred were built in this way between 1929 and 1952. They were treated as expendable and the same running gear might be used several times over. Six similar wagons were built as late as 1963 for the block traffic from Murthwaite to Irton Road, and are still used for PW work.

Tipping wagons. The railway owned at least four small tipping wagons of conventional Hudson contractors' design, and ½ cu yd capacity. They were used around the quarry and Murthwaite yard but are now all scrapped.

Open wagon. A single open wagon with sprung axleboxes was supplied by Theakston about 1933. It may have been a prototype which was not persevered with. The remains were at Murthwaite until recently.

Various oddities.

Dynamometer car. This was definitely of Heywood origin. It was originally a most peculiar four-wheel vehicle with an open body rather higher than it was long, and with a doorless opening at one end. It can be seen on page 133 parked on the short siding by Ravenglass tippler, a position it normally occupied when not in use. A seat was provided across the other end and the recording instruments were fixed on the wagon floor.

There is some confusion about this vehicle but in later years it was either rebuilt as a flat wagon, or the instruments were transferred to a flat wagon—this is the form in which the car is most commonly remembered as working. The instruments consisted basically of a speedometer and revolution counter driven by belting from one axle; and a device for measuring tractive effort. This was done by means of a pressure cylinder fixed under the floor at one end and connected to a long coupling bar which fitted into the ordinary centre coupling on the tender. Readings were recorded on a pressure gauge fixed on the wagon floor.

The wagon in its final state had fallen into decay by the late 1920s and was dismantled. Revolution and speed indicators are still in existence and the cylinder is now used as a valve beneath the water tank at Fisherground!

Heywood special wagons. It is possible that several odd wagons came to Ravenglass, but only one has been identified. It was a short, braked four-wheel vehicle with one end occupied by a wooden box with sloping lid. A transverse seat backed onto the box facing the other end of the wagon which was screened by a waist-high solid bulkhead. It was a most peculiar vehicle and may have been either the 'childrens box wagon' mentioned in the sale catalogue or a workman's tool wagon, of which there were several. At Ravenglass it was rather lightheartedly used on occasion as a mobile shooting butt, the marksman standing in the 'box' while the lid hinged over to lie horizontally, supported on the end bulkhead to form a shelf.

Brocklebank tipping wagon. At an unknown date in the late 20s a remarkable side-tipping wagon was built to designs of Sir Aubrey Brocklebank. It consisted simply of two axle-units carrying wheels and couplers and joined by a single tie-bar, on which a normal V-shape tipper body pivoted: the catches were mounted on the running gear units. The basic idea was sound but a complete failure in service for, when laden, the tipper body bound on the pivots instead of swinging freely. The wagon chassis is still in existence.

To chronicle the changes in goods stock—now used extensively as service vehicles—is rather like trying to hold water in a sieve since wagons can be built and scrapped within only a few years. Of the originals, only two complete granite wagons and bits of tippler wagons survive. A miscellaneous collection of wooden, four-wheeled flats and frames of former bogie coaches are used as required for permanent way purposes and several vehicles have been more permanently converted. Thus components from one of the 1924 four-wheelers form the basis of a stores van, its exterior livery advertising some product (in 1987, Muncaster Mill Flour). *River Irt's* old tender chassis carries a tank. During 1987, the 1928 vintage teak coaches were used generally for PW and service work in the old Mitchell tradition of treating them, seats and all, as wagons. In 1982 a long bogie van, with interior seats and heating was built as a mobile messroom and tool van; it is currently in yellow livery with an Eskdale logo, American style.

Bogie coach dimensions:

Dimension	*Units*	*'Standard' open bogie*	*Jaywick saloons*	*Myers & Bow saloons*
Length over frame	ft in		18 2	23 1
Width overall	ft in	3 9	3 7	3 9
Height ,,	ft in		5 9	5 5
Wheelbase—Total	ft in		15 0	19 0
—Bogie	in	12	12	12
Seating capacity	No	16	8	20

Coach dimensions

		opens		closed	
	1966	1969	1970/1	saloons	semi-opens
length over frame	23′ 4″	20′ 9″	23′ 1″	23′ 9″*	23′ 5″
width overall				3′ 9″	3′ 9″
height overall		varies		5′ 4″	5′ 4″
total wheelbase	17′ 0″	13′ 3″	16′ 6″	17′ 9″*	17′ 0″
bogie wheelbase	2′ 0″	1′ 10″	1′ 10″	1′ 10″	1′ 10″

* early ones are 9″ shorter.

R & E R Coaching Stock List as at November 1987

Key to 'Fittings' codes: B air braked; G guard's compt with handbrake; P piped only; D fitted for disabled passengers; H gas heating; L electric light.

1. *Open Coaches (built R & E R)*

No	*Date*	*Seats*	*Backs*	*Fittings*	*Notes*
1/27	1928	16	low	P	
2/27	,,	16	low	P	
3/27	,,	16	low	P	Wdn as at 11/87
4/27	,,	16	low	P	
5/27	,,	16	low	P	
6/27	,,	16	low	P	
1/66	1966	20	high	P	Myers & Bowman
1/69	1969	20	low	P	4 + 4 + 4 + 4 + 4
2/69	,,	20	low	P	,,
3/69	,,	20	low	P	,,
4/69	,,	20	high	B	,,
1/70	1970	20	high	P	
2/70	,,	20	high	B	
3/70	,,	20	high	B	
1/71	1971	19	low	BG	
2/71	,,	19	low	BG	
3/71	,,	19	low	PG	
1/86	1986	20	high	BG	
1/87	1987	20	high	BG	
2/87	,,	20	high	BG	

Semi Open Coaches

No	*Orig*	*Date*	*Seats*	*Vent*	*Fittings*	*Notes*
101	112	1971	20	–	B	
108	116	1971	20	–	B	
109	118	1974	20	–	B	
116	119	1974	20	–	B	
117	120	1974	20	–	B	
124	121	1974	20	–	B	
125	–	1981	20	–	B	
126	–	1981	20	–	B	4th car DMU 1984
127	–	1982	20	–	PD	
128	–	1982	20	–	PD	
129	–	1982	20	–	PD	

Closed Saloon Coaches

No	*Orig*	*Date*	*Seats*	*Vent*	*Fittings*	*Notes*
102	106	1968	20	louvre	B	
103	107	1968	20	„	B	
104	108	1968	16	„	GP	
105	117	1971	20	hopper	BL	
106	104	1967	20	louvre	P	Myers & Bowman
107	105	1967	20	„	P	„
110	109	1970	20	„	BHL	
111	110	1970	20	„	BHL	
112	113	1970	16	„	GPHL	
113	111	1971	20	„	B	
114	–	1971	20	„	BH	
115	–	1971	20	„	PH	
118	–	1975	20	hopper	B	
119	–	1975	20	„	P	
120	127	1975	16	„	BGL	
121	–	1975	20	„	PL	
122	–	1975	20	„	PL	
123	–	1977	19	„	BLD	r/c disabled saloon
RC1	126	1975	14	hopper	BL	r/c power car
RC2	–	1977	18	„	BL	„ „ „

Appendices

COLONEL YOLLAND'S REPORTS

Ravenglass
29th June, 1876

The Secretary,
Railway Department,
Board of Trade.

Sir,

I have the honour to report for the information of the Board of Trade in compliance with the instructions contained in your Minute of the 20th instant, that I have inspected the Ravenglass and Eskdale Railway from its commencement at Ravenglass Station of the Whitehaven and Furness Junction Railway, to its terminus near the village of Boot, in Eskdale. This Railway was authorised by its special Act to be constructed on any gauge varying from 2 feet 9 inches to 4 feet 8½ inches which might be mentioned by the Board of Trade, and the Department by letter dated 14th March, 1874, sanctions the Company's proposal to construct it on a gauge of 3 feet.

The length of line submitted for inspection is 7 miles and 5 chains, single throughout, with sidings at the commencement and near its termination, and at one intermediate station, Hollowstones, but the land has been purchased for a double line of railway.

The width of the line at formation level is 10 feet for embankments and 9 ft 6 inches for cuttings.

The permanent way consists of a flat bottomed or Vignoles section of rail 3½ inches in depth, and about the same width of bottom flange, weighing 40 lbs per linear yard, in lengths of 15, 18, and 21 feet. This rail is fixed on transverse sleepers, by means of fang-bolts with clips at the joints, and at the centre of each rail, and with jagged dog spikes at the intermediate sleepers. The joints of the rails are fished with two plates and 4—¾ inch bolts to each joint.

The sleepers are partly of larch and partly of Memel timber creosoted, the former are 5 feet 6 inches in length by 9½ inches and 4½ inches, and the latter are 5 feet in length and of the same scantling; they are placed 3 feet 1 inch apart from centre to centre, except at the joints where they are 2 feet 6 inches from centre to centre.

The line is full of sharp curves and steep inclines—the sharpest curve has a radius of 3 chains and the steepest incline is 1 in 40.

The ballast is of broken granite, gravel and sand and stated to be from 4 inches to 1 foot 6 inches in depth below the under sides of the sleepers.

The fencing is partly of the ordinary post (larch) and rail fencing, 4 feet

6 inches in height, and consisting of 4 rails with posts 9 feet apart, and with two intermediate pricks, and partly of wire fencing of the same height, with 7 wires and with posts 6 feet apart, and with rack and pinion brackets for straining wires fixed to straining posts at convenient distances.

There are 7 over and 9 under bridges on the line, all with one exception being of masonry with brick arches or timber beams. The exception has wrought iron girders having a span of about 32 feet on the skew. The girders have sufficient theoretical strength and exhibited a very moderate deflection under the weight of the engine of about 12½ tons in weight.

There are no viaducts or tunnels and no Level Crossings of Public Roads.

Stations have been constructed at Ravenglass, Hollowstones, King of Prussia, and Boot. The platforms are about 1 foot 9 inches in height.

The line has not at the present time been properly completed.

In some of the rock cuttings the rocks have not been cut away sufficiently to allow the doors of the carriages to pass without being carried away and some stone walls, fencing and some trees are also too close to the line. Some of the embankments are built at the outside of dry stone walls nearly perpendicular, these should have greater slopes given to them, in fact made wider at the base: additional ballast which can be used for packing is required throughout, the line having been boxed up with large stones in many cases, at the ends of the sleepers, which will prevent the permanent way men from lifting, regulating and packing the sleepers, until these stones are removed—and this lifting regulating and packing is very much required.

The sides of the cuttings also require cleaning out for the proper drainage of the line.

The stations are incomplete and some of them require shelter to be provided. There are no signals, properly so called on the line, but indicators have or are to be placed above where sidings join the main line to show that the points are properly closed to the stock rails.

Tie rods are required at each end of the longitudinal timbers that carry the rails over the large number of cattle creeps, or over small streams, to preserve the gauge.

There are a large number of occupation level Crossings and the gates require to be fastened by padlock.

The Stations require name boards, clocks, conveniences, and some of them have no shelter at present.

At Boot Station the west end of the platform should be ramped off and the railing removed.

Where the wire fencing is at the side of arable or pasture land, intermediate or prick posts are required, as there were a number of sheep and lambs on the line when I went over it. No arrangements for working on the Block System have been made. No Gradient Boards have been fitted.

I don't recollect having seen anywhere where the masonry was of such indifferent quality.

The Company have not provided any turntables as they contemplate working the traffic with a Tank Engine and they propose to limit the speed to 10 miles an hour with a very much smaller rate round the sharp curves. But the Company has only one Tank Engine and that will not be sufficient.

This engine has 10 inch Cylinders and 16 inch Stroke. It is a six-wheeled coupled Engine weighing with coal and water about 13 tons (sic) and having the weight equal on the leading and trailing wheels. The diameter of the wheels is about 2 feet 9 inches and the length of the wheel base 9 feet 9 inches. The diameter of the Boiler of the Engine is 2 feet 7 inches and its length 7 feet 11 inches.

The Engineer proposes to improve some of the worst curves on the line as they are somewhat sharp for such a length of Wheel Base.

I have now therefore to report that by reason of the incompleteness of the work and the insufficiency of the establishment, the opening of the Ravenglass and Eskdale Railway for traffic cannot be sanctioned without danger to the Public using the same.

I have, etc,

(Signed) W. Yolland
Colonel

Liverpool
9th November, 1876

Sir,

I have the honour to report for the information of the Board of Trade in compliance with the instructions contained in your Minute of the 28th ultimo that I have reinspected the Ravenglass and Eskdale Railway.

The Company have constructed three additional Road-side Stations, Beckton, Eskdale Green and Muncaster and the condition of the line is now very different from what it was when I made my report on the 29th June so that it is now in fair order; but there are still some few places where the embankments are supported by nearly upright dry stone walls and at some of the Stations conveniences have not yet been supplied. The Secretary (Mr Marshall) and Engineer of the Line (Mr Page) have however informed me that these matters shall at once be attended to and completed. In other respects my requirements have been complied with.

The Company have now obtained a second Locomotive Engine and I am of the opinion that the Board of Trade should sanction the opening of the Ravenglass and Eskdale Railway on the following conditions.

1. That only one Engine with train attached to it shall be upon this single line between Ravenglass and Boot Station at one and the same time.

2. That speed on this single line shall not exceed a maximum rate of 10 miles an hour as no attempt has yet been made to get rid of the very sharp curves which were authorised by the Ravenglass and Eskdale Act of 1873.

3. That the traffic shall be worked by Engines having not less than six wheels and whose gross weight when loaded with Coal and water shall not exceed 13 tons.

I have, etc,

(Signed) W. Yolland,
Colonel

A NOTE ON THE GAUGE

In the first edition of this book it was noted that there had long been confusion about the exact gauge of the original R & ER. The problem was that 2 ft 9 in was specified in the 1873 act as the lower limit and there must have been some reason for such an unusual gauge to be specified. In addition, visitors over the years, including Mary C. Fair and Proctor Mitchell, have stated in writing that the gauge was 2 ft 9 in. A special return to the Board of Trade in 1898 also gave this gauge (but then the 'evidence' may well have been taken from the Act).

The case for the 3 ft gauge is that the company did obtain permission from the Board of Trade in 1874 to construct its line to a 3 ft gauge (cf Colonel Yolland's report) and that the maker's drawings for *Devon* were clearly marked 3 ft gauge. In addition a local drawing of *Devon* 'from life' in the 1880s clearly shows the same gauge while various visitors over the years cited this gauge as correct—including Mary C. Fair! Since the book was written evidence, in the form of old sleepers dug up at Ravenglass, has confirmed that the gauge was 3 ft, at least in latter years. Since it is not likely to have been changed while the railway was in existence, this appears conclusive.

A NOTE ON THE SYSTEM OF TRAIN OPERATION BY RADIO CONTROL

The R & ER has pioneered the use of radio in this country as an aid to controlling train operation over single track. The term 'radio control' is commonly used by the company to describe its method of train operation but is really a misnomer. It is, more properly, centralised traffic control using radio instead of telephone or lineside visual signals as a communications medium, and appears to be a blend of British and Continental ideas.

Basically, operation is in the hands of a single controller at Ravenglass who determines what trains, and therefore what paths, are needed; he issues instructions to train crews as appropriate and records his actions on a graphic timetable which shows possible paths, all authorised train movements and all movements actually made, in case of future need. He also records, on tape, all messages between himself and the train crews. For an individual train the procedure is as follows. Shortly before departure time the driver checks that his radio is working and then collects from the controller a train sheet showing the block sections with any scheduled crossings marked; the reverse shows his planned return path. He receives direct verbal clearance to the first section end (eg Miteside loop) and marks it on his sheet with an arrow. On appoaching each section end he reports by radio to the controller at a specified marked reporting point and is given further instructions which are duly marked on his trainsheet. Likewise a train coming to a stop in a loop to allow another to pass reports that it is clear 'inside' and a train entering a section reports the fact to the controller who can then plot it as occupying the section to the next passing loop. *All* messages are repeated as a security measure; all drivers can hear the controller who identifies the train he wants by its call sign, but only the controller can hear the drivers calling in. Loop points are weighted to give a different road for each direction of running.

The line is divided into four absolute block sections, the stations and loops being considered as out-of-section; this enables the controller to pass two following trains through a section in succession, the first being held inside the appropriate loop and the other being authorised to proceed only as far as the reporting board (effectively the home signal) approaching that loop. Various security measures and rules are provided to cover such things as change of instructions and there is a back-up telephone system in case of radio failure. The radio system is fail safe in that a driver is not permitted to proceed into the section ahead until he has received an instruction to do so. If there is a fault in the radio link the drivers cannot receive instructions and thus do not proceed beyond their previously authorised movement until they have called control on the telephones placed at all passing places.

OPERATING DETAILS OF THE 3 ft GAUGE LINE

These details are abstracted from the annual Returns to the Board of Trade made by the R & E and the Eskdale Railway (one year only). As with many such returns their accuracy cannot be guaranteed for small railways had a habit of copying their previous reports where this would save trouble (e.g. stock returns) without reference to the actual situation.

In respect of stock the R & E managers seem to have been very conscien-

	Length	Passengers				Goods	
Year	*in Miles*	*1st*	*3rd/P*	*Total*	*+Seasons*	*Minerals*	*General*
1875	7	—	—	—	—	6,378	387
76	7	96	1,017	1,113	—	9,138	1,164
77	7	861	14,729	15,590	—	7,550	1,300
78	7	741	15,417	16,158	—	5,102	1,584
79	7	747	13,785	14,532	—	4,549	1,077
1880	7	976	20,757	21,733	—	8,719	2,896
81	7	957	18,916	19,873	54	7,317	1,687
82	7	1,235	21,839	23,074	22	4,429	1,960
83	7	739	19,967	20,706	25	1,915	1,606
84	7	551	20,459	21,010	43	1,582	1,619
85	7	395	20,673	21,068	92	22	1,648
86	7	255	18,663	18,918	9	780	675
87	7	314	20,933	21,247	32	538	827
88	7	272	24,377	24,649	29	723	716
89	7	519	24,999	25,518	36	921	756
1890	7	390	25,370	25,760	59	853	810
91	7	308	24,785	25,093	75	1,063	851
92	7	361	25,206	25,567	43	695	677
93	7	390	27,850	28,249	46	803	760
94	7	427	29,583	30,010	53	874	976
95	7	501	29,386	29,887	49	695	896
96	7	220	29,512	29,732	54	879	724
97	7	109	29,293	29,402	59	677	662
98	7	582	27,845	28,427	49	758	608
99	7	537	28,173	28,710	20	632	593
1900	7	595	28,244	28,839	30	587	539
01	7	537	29,378	29,915	62	950	595
02	7	677	28,191	28,868	9	930	635
03	7	907	31,485	32,392	12	1,076	780
04	7	966	30,750	31,716	5	980	810
05	7	576	29,477	30,053	3	784	537
06	7	805	28,387	29,192	3	935	535
07	7	702	28,880	29,582	4	796	527
08	7	591	23,819	24,410	4	996	461
09	Line officially closed to traffic from 30.11.08						
1910	7+1	—	—	—	—	1,399	

tious, the fluctuation between 'goods vehicles' and 'other purposes' apparently depending on how many wagons were serviceable at the particular time. The only obvious error is the number of passenger vans in the 1880 returns, the B o T clerk clearly having misread an elaborate '1' for a '4'.

Otherwise, the figures speak for themselves. The only point of note is that, from 1896 on, coinciding with a change of manager, it would appear that general coal traffic, etc, was transferred from the 'Minerals' column to 'general' goods.

Receipts (£)			*Total*	*Op*	*Stock*			
Pass.	*Goods*	*Total*	*Expen.*	*Ratio*	*L*	*C*	*PV*	*W*
—	1,011	1,011	442	44	1	2	1	31
27	1,517	1,544	1,267	82	2	2	1	31+2
393	1,188	1,581	1,473	93	2	3	1	24+9
420	749	1,169	1,177	101	2	3	1	30+4
380	584	964	900	93	2	3	-	34
532	1,389	1,921	1,817	95	2	3	4	24+9
538	874	1,412	1,316	93	2	3	1	28+9
602	611	1,213	1,050	87	2	3	-	29
551	386	937	833	89	2	3	1	29
564	313	877	893	102	2	3	-	19
575	230	805	847	105	2	3	-	19
527	188	715	707	99	2	3	1	18
544	206	750	729	97	2	3	1	19
630	201	831	748	90	2	3	1	19
694	226	920	858	93	2	3	1	19
732	228	960	921	96	2	3	1	19
715	251	966	963	100		„		
752	188	940	935	99		„		
807	222	1,029	1,012	98		„		
865	255	1,120	1,034	92		„		
825	234	1,059	1,056	100		„		
832	215	1,047	1,281	122	2	3	1	14
838	191	1,029	1,054	102	2	3	1	11+7
848	200	1,048	1,207	115	2	3	1	19+8
838	178	1,016	1,100	108	2	3	1	10+8
867	164	1,031	1,084	105		„		
907	205	1,112	1,158	104		„		
858	282	1,140	1,186	—	2	3	1	11+7
955	264	1,219	1,215	100		„		
956	258	1,214	1,267	—		„		
915	276	1,191	1,151	97	2	3	1	10+8
881	274	1,155	1,137	98	2	3	1	11+7
880	253	1,133	1,212	—	2	3	1	11+7
759	242	1,001	1,318	—	2	3	1	11+1
—	—	89	108	—				
—	207	207	225	—	1	-	-	8

THE ESKDALE (CUMBRIA) TRUST AND THE RAILWAY MUSEUM

It has been clear for some years that there are several activities which would much enhance the railway's surroundings but which the company cannot reasonably be expected to fund. In 1977, therefore, Lord Wakefield set up the Eskdale (Cumbria) Trust as a non-profit making organisation to work in collaboration with the railway company. Its intention is to preserve and encourage interest in the historical aspects of Eskdale and so far it has initiated two major projects. The first is the old water mill at Muncaster which has been restored to working order and opened to the public since 1977. The second is a small museum of the railway which was opened to contain the large number of relics collected for the Centenary Exhibition of 1976. Opened in 1978, the Museum is currently housed in the old down-line shelter on Ravenglass (BR) station, modified and extended to suit its new purpose. It contains a reproduction of an old mine gallery, detailed displays of models, relics and photographs of the 3 ft and 15 in gauge lines and a section devoted to granite quarrying. At present full-size static exhibits are restricted to a Bassett Lowke coach, various wagons and a Class 30 Bassett Lowke Atlantic *Synolda,* formerly of the 15 in gauge Sand Hutton Railway. *Synolda* is almost identical to *Sans Pareil* and was painstakingly restored to working order by apprentices of British Nuclear Fuels Ltd in 1980. She is currently painted in NGR blue livery and is occasionally used for special workings.

TIMETABLES

To record all the small variations in R & E timetables would require a complete book and this appendix will be confined to general notes. Specimen timetables for typical years are included for those who want to study the minutiae.

1876 - 1908

Apart from the years 1876 and 1877, when three trains daily were run in summer and two in winter, the R & E timetables basically constituted five trains daily on weekdays in summer and three in the winter, with an additional early morning train in winter on Thursdays only; Thursday was Whitehaven market day. Three Sunday trains were provided in summer for tourists, but there was no winter Sunday service. Except for a few years in the 1870s and early 80s, when separate goods trains were run, all trains were mixed.

Exact times of services varied over the years, presumably owing to variations in the timetables of the Furness Railway, with which connections were made. Representative years are shown below; the main points of interest are the adjustment to the needs of tourists, in the 1899 timetable, and the termination of the last evening train at Beckfoot, a measure instituted in the early 1890s.

Extra services were regularly run at bank holidays, normally requiring the addition of a 6.30 pm working from Ravenglass, together with a sparse Sunday service (Easter) and the addition to the summer schedules of an early further morning train at Whit, August Bank Holiday, and Fell Dales Show. A typical abbreviated timetable is shown below. It will be noted that, while times allowed the service to be run by one train only, turn-round times were extremely short at both ends and it is almost certain that both engines would be in steam on such occasions, one taking over from the other at Ravenglass. Specimen tables are given below.

Summer 1878			*Weekdays*				*Sundays*	
UP								
Ravenglass	8.35	10.30	12.30	4.30	8.05	10.00	4.00	6.15
Muncaster	8.40	—	12.35	4.35	8.10	10.05	4.05	6.20
Irton Road	8.50	10.50	12.55	4.50	8.25	10.20	4.20	6.35
Eskdale Green	9.00	—	1.05	4.55	8.30	10.25	4.25	6.40
Beckfoot	9.15	—	1.25	5.20	8.45	10.40	4.40	6.55
Boot	9.20	11.10	1.30	5.25	8.50	10.45	4.45	7.00
DOWN								
Boot	9.30	11.20	2.10	5.30	8.55	12.05	5.00	7.15
Beckfoot	9.35	11.25	2.15	5.35	9.00	12.10	5.05	7.25
Eskdale Green	9.50	11.40	2.35	5.50	9.15	12.25	5.20	7.30
Irton Road	10.00	11.45	2.45	6.00	9.20	12.35	5.30	7.40
Muncaster	10.15	12.00	3.05	6.15	9.35	12.50	5.45	7.55
Ravenglass	10.20	12.05	3.10	6.20	9.40	12.55	5.50	8.00

Winter 1880-1 (shortened version. All trains stop at all stations)

		Weekdays only			
Ravenglass	dep	6.30	8.35	12.15	4.32
Boot	arr	7.15	9.20	1.05	5.15
Boot	dep	7.25	9.30	2.10	5.30
Ravenglass	arr	8.15	10.15	3.10	6.20

Summer 1889 (from FR timetable)

		Weekdays					*Sundays*		
Ravenglass	dep	6.45	9.35	12.10	3.10	6.30	9.40	3.00	6.25
Boot	arr	7.30	10.20	12.55	3.55	7.10p	10.25	3.45	7.05p
Boot	dep	7.35	10.45	2.05	4.45	7.20p	12.20	5.15	7.10p
Ravenglass	arr	8.20	11.30	2.50	5.30	8.00	1.10	6.00	7.50

p=Beckfoot

1904. *Special timetable for Fell Dales Show* (28/9); Whitehaven News

Ravenglass	dep	6.35	8.25	10.05	12.20	3.10	5.45
Boot	dep	7.25	9.15	10.55	1.55	4.40	7.15

1915–25

Apart from the initial years 1915-16, when timetables altered as the line was extended and more locomotives and stock became available, the basic summer service comprised six to seven trains on weekdays with either three or four trains on Sundays. The winter service comprised an early morning and an evening train up and down the dale on weekdays only.

Specimen tables are given below. One point somewhat confusing to the uninitiated is the starting of the first train and termination of the last one at Irton Road, except on Saturdays. The explanation is that Mitchell and many of the staff lodged there and it was in effect a staff train! A locomotive or tractor was stabled overnight in the small shed there. The train was extended to Beckfoot on Saturdays to serve guests arriving at the CHA

Stanley Ghyll centre. The 1924 table shows also the 11.30 and 12.30 ex-Ravenglass obviously crossing down trains at Murthwaite.

1 *July* 1919 *until further notice*

	Weekdays						*Sundays*			
Ravenglass	8.30	11.15	12.35	3.05	6.45	7.30	9.30	11.20	2.00	6.15
Muncaster	8.35	—	12.40	3.10	6.50	7.35	9.35	11.25	2.05	6.20
Irton Rd	8.55	—	1.00	3.30	7.05	7.55	9.55	11.45	2.25	6.40
Eskdale Gn	9.00	—	1.05	3.35	Not	8.00	10.00	11.50	2.30	6.45
Beckfoot	9.15	12.00	1.20	3.50	Sats	8.15	10.15	12.05	2.45	7.00
						Sats				
						only				
Beckfoot	9.40	1.30	3.10	4.50	6.00		10.25		4.50	7.15
Eskdale Gn	9.50	1.40	3.20	5.00	6.10		10.35		5.00	7.25
Irton Rd	10.00	1.50	3.30	5.10	6.20		10.45		5.10	7.35
Muncaster	10.15	2.05	3.45	5.25	6.35		11.00		5.25	7.50
Ravenglass	10.25	2.15	3.55	5.35	6.45		11.10		5.35	8.00

Timetable from 2 June 1924 until further notice
This service will not be in operation on Whit Monday, 9 June

		Weekdays							*Sundays*			
Ravenglass	dep	8.00	9.45	11.20	12.30	1.50	4.00	6.30		11.00	2.15	7.00
Muncaster		x	x	x	x	x	x	x		x	x	x
Irton Road		8.30	10.10	11.45	12.55	2.20	4.25	6.55		11.25	2.40	7.25
Eskdale Green		8.45	10.15	11.50	1.00	2.25	4.30	7.00+		11.30	2.45	
Beckfoot		9.05	10.30	12.05	1.15	2.40	4.45	7.15+		11.40	2.55	
Dalegarth		9.15	10.35	12.10	1.20	2.45	4.50	7.20+		11.45	3.00	
Dalegarth	dep	9.40	11.00	12.10	2.00	3.00	4.50			12.05	3.30	5.35
Beckfoot		9.50	11.02	12.12	2.02	3.02	4.52			12.07	3.32	5.37
Eskdale Green		10.00	11.15	12.25	2.15	3.15	5.05			12.20	3.45	5.50
Irton Road	8.40	10.10	11.20	12.30	2.20	3.20	5.10		9.15	12.25	3.50	6.00
Muncaster	z	z	z	z	z	z	z		z	z	z	z
Ravenglass	9.05	10.35	11.50	1.05	2.45	3.45	5.35		9.40	12.50	4.15	6.30

\+ Saturdays only
x Will call at Muncaster if required 5 min after leaving Ravenglass to pick up passengers for Irton Road and beyond only
z Will stop to set down passengers if notice is given to the Guard before leaving Irton Road

1926–39

The new régime started off confidently with a similar summer timetable of six trains each way plus one short working extended on Saturdays, and two to three trains on Sundays. During the 1930s, published timetables became very complicated as can be seen from the specimen sheet, and the basic service offered only four trains a day. Complications were increased by the practice of issuing one comprehensive sheet for the whole season instead of the series of sheets favoured by Mitchell. Interesting features of this period are the retention of Thursdays-only market day workings and unbalanced workings on both weekdays and Sundays. The latter involved a gathering of trains at Dalegarth, the 2.25 ex-Ravenglass on Sunday invariably being double-headed or working in more than one section. The winter service, still of two daily trains on weekdays only, was reduced after 1927-8 to Thursdays only and appears to have been discontinued after the 1936-7 winter.

Timetable 8 July, 1935, until further notice
This timetable will not be in operation on August Bank Holiday Monday, 5 August, 1935. A Special Full Service of Trains will be run on this day connecting with LMS Excursions and Ordinary Trains from Ravenglass

		Weekdays								*Sundays until Sept 15*		
Ravenglass	dep	7a20	9b25	10c55	11b 5	12.30	3. 5	4b20	6*50	11.45	2.20	
Irton Road		7a40	9b45	11c15	11b25	12.50	3.25	4b40	7*10	12. 5	2.40	
Eskdale Green		7a45	9b50	11c20	11b30	12.55	3.30	4b45	7*15	12.10	2.45	
Beckfoot**		7a55	10b 5	11c35	11b45	1.10	3.45	4b55	7*25	12.25	3.0	
Dalegarth	arr	8a 0	10b10	11c40	11b50	1.15	3.50	5b 0	7*30	12.30	3. 5	
Dalegarth	dep	8a 5	10b15	11c50	11b55	2. 5		5. 5	8*00	12.35	5. 0	6.45
Beckfoot !		8a 7	10b17	11c52	11b57	2. 7		5. 7	8*02	12.37	5.02	6.47
Eskdale Green		8a15	10b30	12c00	12c 5	2.15		5.15	8*10	12.45	5.10	6.55
Irton Road		8a20	10b35	12c05	12b10	2.20		5.20	8*15	12.50	5.15	7.0
Ravenglass	arr	8a45	11b 0	12c25	12b30	2.40		5.45	8*35	1.10	5.40	7.20

** Stops to set down only. ! Stops to pick up only. * Will not run after Sept 7th. a—Runs Thursdays only. b—Runs Saturdays only. c—Runs Daily except Saturday.

RAVENGLASS & ESKDALE RAILWAY

TIME TABLE.

JULY 3rd until SEPTEMBER 22nd, 1939.

This Time Table will not be in operation on August Monday, August 7th, 1939. A Special Service of Trains will operate on that day, connecting with L.M.S. Excursion Trains.

‡—Stops to set down
§—Stops to pick up

	WEEK-DAYS.							SUNDAYS.		
	a.m. (Runs Thursdays only)	a.m. (Runs Saturdays only)	a.m.	p.m.	p.m.	p.m. (Runs Sats only)	p.m.	a.m. (Runs until Sept. 10th only)	p.m. (Runs until Sept. 10th only)	p.m. (Runs until Sept. 10th only)
Ravenglass dep.	*7 40*	*9 30*	10a55	12a30	3 c 5	*4 20*	6 d55	11 45	2 25	
Irton Road ...	*8 0*	*9 50*	11a15	12a50	3 c 25	*4 40*	7 d15	12 5	2 45	
Eskdale Green...	*8 3*	*9 55*	11a20	12a55	3 c 30	*4 45*	7 d20	12 10	2 50	
Beckfoot ‡ ...	*8 10*	*10 10*	11a35	1 a10	3 c 45	*4 55*	7 d30	12 25	3 5	
Dalegarth arr.	*8 15*	*10 15*	11a40	1 a15	3 c 50	*5 0*	7 d35	12 30	3 10	
Dalegarth dep.	*8 20*	*10 20*	11a45	2 b 0	...	5 5	7 e45	12 35	5 0	6 45
Beckfoot § ...	*8 22*	*10 25*	11a47	2 b 2	...	5 7	7 e47	12 37	5 2	6 47
Eskdale Green...	*8 30*	*10 35*	11a55	2 b 10	...	5 15	7 e55	12 45	5 10	6 55
Irton Road ...	*8 35*	*10 40*	12a 0	2 b 15	...	5 20	8 e 0	12 50	5 15	7 0
Ravenglass arr.	*8 55*	*11 0*	12a20	2 b 40	...	5 45	8 e20	1 10	5 40	7 20

a—Runs 10 mins. later on Sats. and 30 mins. later on Thursday, until September 7th.
b—Runs 40 mins. earlier leaving Dalegarth at 1-20 p.m. on Wednesdays July 5th and 19th, August 2nd, 16th, and 30th, and September 13th. c—Will not run on Saturdays, September 9th and 16th.
d—Runs daily until September 2nd. Saturdays only after September 2nd.
e—Runs daily except Saturdays until September 1st.

Narrow Gauge Railways, Limited,
W. GILLON,
General Manager, RAVENGLASS.

87.

1946–60

Services after the war were very sparse for some years, consisting only of two trains each way daily, including Sundays, with one or two additional trains on Saturdays and Wednesdays. Exact times varied but there was normally a morning train from Ravenglass at about 11 am and an afternoon one about 2.15

After 1953, a fairly standard service was run with three to four basic

RAVENGLASS & ESKDALE RAILWAY

Visit Eskdale by the Wonderful Miniature Railway.

SUMMER TIME TABLE.

JUNE 11th, 1956 UNTIL FURTHER NOTICE.

		WEEK-DAYS									SUNDAY			
			S. O. a.m.	a.m.	p.m.	p.m.	S. E. p.m.	S. O. p.m.	S. E. p.m.	S.O. p.m.	a.m.	p.m.	p.m.	p.m.
Ravenglass	dep.	...	9-05	11-25	1-0	2-40	4-25	4-25	6-25	6-25	11-25	2-30	3-0	4-30
Irton Road	...	...	...	11-45	1-20	3-0	...	4-45	6-45	6-45	11-45	2-50	3-20	4-50
Eskdale Green	...	...	...	11-50	1-25	3-5	...	4-50	STOP	6-50	11-50	2-55	3-25	4-55
Beckfoot *	...	...	...	12-05	1-40	3-20	...	5-0		7-0	12-05	3-10	3-35	5-5
Dalegarth	arr.	...	9-40	12-10	1-45	3-25	5-0	5-5		7-5	12-10	3-15	3-40	5-10
			S. O.	p.m.	p.m.	p.m.	p.m.	p.m.			p.m.		p.m.	p.m.
Dalegarth	dep.	...	9-50	12-15	1-50	3-35	5-5	5-15	...	...	12-15	...	3-45	5-15
Beckfoot †	...	...	9-55	12-17	1-52	...	...	5-17	...	...	12-17	...	3-47	5-17
Eskdale Green	...	...	10-05	12-25	2-0	...	...	5-25	...	...	12-25	...	3-55	5-25
Irton Road	...	8-0	10-10	12-30	2-5	...	...	5-30	...	...	12-30	...	4-0	5-30
Ravenglass	arr.	8-20	10-35	12-55	2-30	4-15	5-45	5-55	...	...	12-55	...	4-20	5-55

S. E. Sats. Excepted. S. O. Sats. Only * Stops to set down only. † Stops to pick up only.

This Time Table will not be in operation BANK HOLIDAY MONDAY and TUESDAY, AUGUST 6th and 7th. A Special Service of Trains will run these days as required. Special Trains can be arranged for large parties; for fares and particulars apply to:

THE GENERAL MANAGER,
RAVENGLASS & ESKDALE RAILWAY,
RAVENGLASS, Cumberland.

Phone: Ravenglass 26.

trains on weekdays and Sundays, additional workings being provided on Saturdays. An interesting feature was the revival of the morning and evening short workings from and to Irton Road, and the revival of unbalanced workings on Sundays. Several workings were non-stop 'expresses'.

For the last season under Keswick Granite control the service was simplified to four workings each way on weekdays with an extra morning train on Saturdays, and two afternoon trains only on Sundays with an additional up train only in the high season.

1961–on

The new company operated a similar timetable to the 1960 one during its first season but since then has increased and refined the service to cope with increasing traffic. An early development was the re-introduction, in the winter of 1960-61, of a Mon-Fri service leaving Dalegarth at 7.45 am and returning from Ravenglass at about 4.30 pm (times vary slightly from year to year). This is really a staff train but does provide a means of transport for valley residents who want a day out!

The other main development has been the perfecting of the 'shuttle service' whereby a train can be dispatched up the valley every 50 min at peak periods, running in several portions if required. At all other periods of the 15 in gauge, normal timetables were suspended at peak periods, but the administrative arrangements now make it possible to operate the shuttle at very short notice if traffic requires.

Timetable for Summer 1961

	Weekdays					*Sundays*		
Ravenglass	9.05	11.20	12.55	2.40	4.35	2.30	3.00	4.30
Irton Road	*	11.40	1.15	3.00	4.55	2.50	3.20	4.50
Eskdale Green	*	11.45	1.20	3.05	5.00	2.55	3.25	4.55
Beckfoot " (arr)	*	12.00	1.35	3.20	5.15	3.10	3.35	5.05
Dalegarth	9.40 (SO)	12.05	1.40	3.25	5.20	3.15	3.40	5.10
Dalegarth	9.50	12.10	1.45	3.35	5.20		3.45	5.15
Beckfoot'	9.55	12.12	1.47	*	5.22		3.47	5.17
Eskdale Green	10.05	12.20	1.55	*	5.30		3.55	5.25
Irton Road	10.10	12.25	2.00	*	5.35		4.00	5.30
Ravenglass	10.35 (SO)	12.50	2.25	4.15	6.00		4.20	5.55

SO—Saturdays only * Stops on request
" Stops to set down only ' Stops to pick up only

Trains will run for Easter, Good Friday to Easter Monday (inclusive) as per above timetable. A special service may operate at busy periods, including Bank Holidays. Extra trains, if available, can be run for private parties if scheduled service unsuitable. Reduced rates for parties booked in advance.

RAVENGLASS & ESKDALE RAILWAY — TIME TABLE, 1966

Return Fares:— Adult - 6/-. Child - 3/-.

Miles			WINTER & SPRING: Jan. 3 to May 13, ex. Easter, and Oct. 17 to Dec. 23 — Mon.—Fri.		WINTER & SPRING: Apr. 13 to May 13 — Wed. & Fri. Only		SUMMER: Easter (April 8th to 11th inclusive) and May 14th to October 1st, inclusive — Daily—including Sundays.									
			a.m.	p.m.	a.m.	p.m.	a.m.	a.m.	a.m. Sat. Only	a.m. Not Sat.	p.m.	p.m.	p.m. A	p.m.	p.m. B	p.m. C
0	Ravenglass	dep.		4.30	11.20	2.40			11.00	11.20	1.00	2.40	3.30	4.20	6.10	7.45
4¼	Irton Road	dep.		5.00	11.40	3.00			11.20	11.40	1.20	3.00	3.50	4.40	6.30	8.05
4¾	Eskdale Green	dep.		*	*	*			11.25	11.45	*	*	*	4.45	*	*
6½	Beckfoot	arr.		sd	sd	sd			sd	sd	sd	sd	sd	sd	sd	sd
7	Dalegarth	arr.		5.15	12.00	3.20			11.40	12.00	1.40	3.20	4.10	5.00	6.45	8.20
							Not Sat.	Sat. Only	Sat. Only	Not Sat.			A	B	C	
0	Dalegarth	dep.	7.45		12.15	3.35	7.45	9.45	11.55	12.15	1.55	3.35	4.25	5.15	6.55	
½	Beckfoot	dep.	pu		pu	pu	pu	9.48	11 58	pu	pu	pu	pu	pu	pu	
2¼	Eskdale Green	dep.	*		*	*	*	*	12.05	12.25	*	*	4.35	5.25	*	
2¾	Irton Road	dep.	8.00		12.30	3.50	8.00	10.00	12.10	12.30	2.10	3.50	4.40	5.30	7.10	
7	Ravenglass	arr.	8.20		12.55	4.15	8 20	10.20	12.35	12.55	2.35	4.15	5.05	5.55	7.30	

NOTES

A Runs July 4th to September 3rd (Connects with 17.27 train from Ravenglass for Whitehaven and Carlisle).

B Runs 10 minutes later from May 14th to July 3rd and from September 4th to October 1st.

C Runs July 4th to September 2nd, Monday to Saturday (Connects with 19.38 train from Ravenglass to Barrow Sleeping Cars to London Euston).

* Stops on Request.

Note: There are no B.R. services from Ravenglass on Sunday.

sd Trains stop on request to the Guard to set-down only.

pu Trains stop on request to pick-up only.

A special service will operate at busy periods.

TIME TABLE SUBJECT TO ALTERATION WITHOUT NOTICE.

Bethwaites, Cleator Moor.

SPECIMEN WORKING TIMETABLE FOR 1924

The text of a Working Timetable for Autumn 1924 has recently come to light and is reproduced here to show how the line was operated. The original is an 11 page printed booklet obviously designed for use at all seasons as paths are provided for all trains likely to be needed even at peak periods. It is interesting to note that, in contrast to present-day practice, 'UP' was regarded as being in the direction of Ravenglass and 'DOWN' trains ran up the valley. Two of the original pages are reproduced on each page here. The larger figures in several places indicate crossings, and in this connection the use of Eskdale Green for the purpose will be noted, together with the stabling of a stone train there overnight.

The cover is reproduced below:

No. 8.

Ravenglass & Eskdale Railway.

WORKING TIME TABLE,

SEPT. 22nd, 1924,

Until Further Notice.

SPECIAL NOTICE to DRIVERS and GUARDS.

All Passenger Trains must carry a Disc at Base of Funnel of Engine and a Disc on Rear Coach of Train. If Train is running in one portion only the Discs will be White. If in two or more portions, the first portion or portions will carry Red Discs and the last portion the White Discs. All Drivers must observe what Discs are carried by the Trains that they pass or that pass them and regulate their movements accordingly.

Great care must be taken in approaching Murthwaite Loop and Murthwaite Crushing Plant. Drivers must whistle on approaching Murthwaite Engine House.

1

SPECIAL NOTICE.

Trains No. 12, 13, 24, 7, and 19 will not run on Saturdays. Engine of Train No. 13 will return to Ravenglass, or to Irton Road if stationed there, arriving not later than 12-25 o'clock at Ravenglass, or 12-20 at Irton Road.

SUNDAY TRAINS.

Train No. 4.............. Clear Road.

Train No. 9.............. Clear Road.

WORKING TIME TABLE.

September 22nd, 1924, until Further Notice.

DOWN TRAINS.

Train No.	1 ~~Emp. Stock~~	3 Pass	5	7 Stone	9	11 Pass	15 Stone	17 Pass
Ravenglass	Light Engine	8 5		—		11 5	—	12 30
Muncaster		Pass		—		Pass	—	Pass
Murthwaite Loop		8 19		9 45		Pass	12 15	12 45
Irton Road. arr.		8 35		9 55		11 30	12 25	12 53
" " dep.	8·20	8 40						12 55
Eskdale Green	8·25	8 45		10 0		11 35	12 30	1 0
Quarry		9 0		10 15		Pass	12 45	Pass
Beckfoot		9 5		—		11 50	—	1 15
Dalegarth		9 10		—		11 55	—	1 20

DOWN TRAINS (continued).

Train No.		19 Stone	21		25 Pass	27	29	31 Pass
Ravenglass		—			4 5			6 30
Muncaster		—			Pass			Pass
Murthwaite Loop		3 0			Pass			Pass
Irton Road, arr.		3 10			4 30			7 0
" " dep.								
Eskdale Green		3 15			4 35			—
Quarry		3 30			Pass			—
Beckfoot		—			4 50			—
Dalegarth		—			4 55			—

WORKING TIME TABLE.

September 22nd, 1924, until Further Notice.

UP TRAINS.

Train No.	2 Stone	4 Pass	6	8 Stone	10	12 Stone	14	16	18
Dalegarth	—	—	9 45	—		—			
Beckfoot, arr...... dep......	—	—	9 50	—		—			
Quarry	—	—	Pass	10 45		1 30			
Eskdale Green....	8 30	—	10 0	11 0		1 45			
Irton Road, arr...	8·35								
" " dep.	8 45	8 40	10 5	11 5		1 50			
Murthwaite Loop	9 0	Pass	Pass	11 15		2 0			
Muncaster	—	Pass	Pass	—		—			
Ravenglass	—	9 5	10 30	—		—			

UP TRAINS (continued).

Train No.	20 Pass	22 Pass	24 Stone	26	28 Pass	30	32 S.O.	34	36 Emp. Stock
Dalegarth	2 5	3 0	—		5 0				
Beckfoot, arr... .. dep.....	2 10	3 5	—		5 5				
Quarry...............	Pass	Pass	4 15		Pass				
Eskdale Green....	2 20	3 15	4 30		5 15				
Irton Road, arr... " " dep...	2 25	3 20	4 40		5 20				
Murthwaite Loop	Pass	Pass	—		Pass				
" "									
Muncaster	Pass	Pass	—		Pass				
Ravenglass	2 50	3 45	—		5 45				

SUNDAYS: UP Trains.

Train No.	1 Pass	3	5 Pass	7	9 Pass	
Dalegarth					5 0	
Beckfoot...........					5 5	
Quarry					Pass	
Eskdale Green ...					5 15	
Irton Road.........					5 20	
Murthwaite Loop					Pass	
Muncaster					Pass	
Ravenglass					5 45	

SUNDAYS: DOWN Trains.

Train No.	2	4 Pass	6	8 Pass	10	12 Pass
Ravenglass		10 45				
Muncaster..........		Pass				
Murthwaite Loop		Pass				
Irton Road.........		11 10				
Eskdale Green....		11 15				
Quarry.............		Pass				
Beckfoot............		11 30				
Dalegarth		11 35				

8

GENERAL INSTRUCTIONS.

Train No. 2. Will not leave Irton Road until Train No. 3 has arrived.

Train No. 3. Stops at Murthwaite, if required, to drop men and pick up trucks. Shunts into siding at Irton Road to allow Trains No. 2 and 4 to pass on main line.

Train No. 4. Leaves Irton Road after arrival of Train No. 3. Clear Road to Ravenglass.

Train No. 6. Shunts into siding at Eskdale Green to allow Train No. 7 to pass on main line.

Train No. 7. Passes on main line Train No. 6 in siding at Eskdale Green.

Train No. 8. Clear Road to Murthwaite.

Train No. 11. Must not pass Murthwaite until Train No. 8 has arrived. Runs to October 31st only.

Train No. 12. Clear Road. Must not leave Quarry until Train No. 17 has passed.

Train No. 15. Clear Road.

Train No. 17. Passes Train No. 12 in Quarry Siding.

Train No. 19. Passes on main line at Eskdale Green Train No. 22 in siding.

Train No. 20 Clear Road. Pick up trucks if required for Murthwaite.

9

Train No. 22 Shunts into Siding at Eskdale Green to allow Train No. 19 to pass on main line.

Train No. 24. Passes on main line at Eskdale Green Train No. 25 in Siding.

Train No. 25. Shunts into Siding at Eskdale Green to allow Train No. 24 to pass on main line.

Train No. 28. Clear Road.

Train No. 31. Clear Road.

Train No. 1. Light Engine from Irton Rd to pick up stone train at Eskdale Green.

Train No. 24. Shunts into siding at Eskdale Green to allow Train No. 25 to Pass on Main Line. Stone train to be left in siding and engine only to proceed to Irton Rd.

Train No. 25. Passes on Main Line at Eskdale Green. Train No. 24 in siding.

A TECHNICAL DESCRIPTION OF THE ROUTE

from 3 ft gauge to the present

Note: this description tries to reconcile the variations inevitably produced by the 3 ft gauge line followed by, effectively, a succession of modifications and realignments on the 15 inch gauge. The original trackbed is wide enough to have allowed considerable modification of line and level and this continues. The description should be read in conjunction with the atlas and gradient profile, though it must be said the latter is now inaccurate in places.

ENVIRONS OF RAVENGLASS

The Ravenglass station site has always been to the east of the former Furness Railway (latterly BR) goods yard and is split in two by a sunken road that climbs from Ravenglass village to the main coast highway. The 3 ft gauge layout was simple, consisting basically of two dead-end sidings, one of which paralleled a standard gauge line, the other running through a short overall roof covering the wooden, single-storey station building. There was no loop and the sidings were on a falling grade from the road underbridge to allow gravity shunting. North of the bridge, trailing spurs gave access to a stone-built 2-road engine shed and fitters' shop on the east while a transhipment siding ran back on the west from near a still existing house called Raven Villa. This siding rose on an embankment to cross the road at a higher level and straddle a standard gauge siding but there is some doubt if the arrangement was ever complete; OS maps of the 1890s show track terminating north of the road bridge and photos of the same period show rubbish dumped between the supporting walls and a fence across the track further up. Certainly in later years stone was simply dumped in the yard until reloaded.

The 15-inch gauge initially took over the layout, putting in a loop and sidings, utilising existing buildings and storing derelict 3 ft gauge stock on the transhipment bank. The Atlas shows major changes but, briefly, the old transhipment facilities were resuscitated for granite traffic from 1922-3, using a planked gantry and rotary wagon tippler, while the station area was reconstructed piecemeal with new, clap-board buildings including a bungalow for the manager and a carriage shed. The engine shed was enlarged, partly in reinforced concrete, partly with a wood and corrugated iron extension on the north end—which blew down in a gale during the late '20s and was not rebuilt. By 1930 a standard gauge connection to Murthwaite (see Ch. 4) had been built on the flattened site of former transhipment arrangements using a lower bridge and with a loop and engine shelter on the north side. A metal chute beside the engine shed was retained for loading road lorries from the 15 inch gauge since Murthwaite did not have road access and a weighbridge siding was put in alongside the shed—the niche was still visible in 1987. The track layout suffered various upheavals (see Atlas) but otherwise the scene remained essentially the same until the early 1960s. At that period the new company severed the standard gauge connection and, over succeeding years, built a new carriage shed on its site while reusing the bridge girders to replace rotted ones on the original 15 inch gauge line. A pair of BR pullman camping coaches, removed in 1965, were returned to their original position on purchase by the R & E R in 1969, just before the old goods yard was dismantled. This has since become a carpark though the coaches remain as summer 'lets' to confuse unwary visitors. The former Furness Railway buildings have become R & E R property as a pub, a museum and a workshop and of late further alterations have taken place as described in Ch. 8. Since 1969 the station has also been fully signalled with main points interlocked and worked from a signal box which also houses the traffic controller.

RAVENGLASS – MUNCASTER MILL

From Raven Villa, the single track runs along the original trackbed north east and then eastward. From here Railway No 2 of the 3 ft gauge—never built—would have run back along the river bank and under the main line railway to terminate 'on the sea shore at a point in front of Ravenglass village'. Here, too, first the 15 inch gauge, and later the standard gauge transhipment links joined the main line, the SG straddling the 15 inch gauge right up to Murthwaite; it joined and left via ingenious crossings with swivelling sections and guarded by crude lower quadrant semaphore signals. The line undulates across Barrow Marsh and then dives beneath the coast road to run into Muncaster Mill halt on a falling left-hand curve. The 3 ft gauge had a simple stone-faced platform here with one of its standard wooden shelter-cum-booking huts, the early 15 inch gauge using the facilities until they fell down. In recent years the railway has installed a platform and a relief siding, facing to Ravenglass, while in 1987 a neat stone shelter was erected for use by visitors to the mill.

MUNCASTER MILL TO IRTON ROAD

The following section through Mill Wood marks the start of a climb that, if undulating at times, lasts almost to the half way point of Irton Road. At just over one and a half miles is Miteside Halt, a conditional stop noted in 3 ft gauge days for its shelter formed from an old skiff and serving only Miteside House and a few scattered farms;

in 1975, part of an old boat was again set up as a shelter here. Shortly after the halt, the line reaches the first of three passing loops required by modern operating methods. Left-hand running is practised and the weighted points are protected by a modern version of Quan's patent point indicator.

The next point of note is Murthwaite crushing plant, or rather its remains, tucked under the fellside. This was always rail-served since it has never had proper road access. In 3 ft gauge days attempts were made to quarry stone here but success came only in the early 1920s when the crushing plant was built and a quarry opened just to the east of it. From 1922 to the early 1950s the site was definitely industrial, with loops, sidings and considerable desecration of the landscape; it also, for many years housed the railway's workshops. Since its closure, however, the buildings have been demolished and the ruins are steadily being reclaimed by nature; many passengers never realise there was a quarry here at all.

From Murthwaite, the line climbs steadily along the fellside, Horsefalls Wood to the north of Raven Crag towering high to the south. The line is here quite high above the River Mite on that man-made ledge which so incurred Colonel Yolland's censure when he first walked the line. Certainly at that much photographed spot Rock Point (just over 3¼ miles) it is high enough for one not to wish to be on a drystone sheer retaining wall and one is grateful that Mr Quan agreed to build up the embanking to a more stable slope with earth and rubble. There follows another potential trouble spot, the steep Walk Mill bank which leads to the first real easement at Walk Mill summit—and from there the line drops away sharply into a dip by the 'big stone' before rising dead-straight through the abutments of a former 3 ft gauge accommodation bridge to the main intermediate station of Irton Road at the lower end of Eskdale Green village. The 3 ft gauge initially called it Hollowstones and had a goods siding here, with a quite substantial stone-built shelter and booking office fronting a stone-faced platform by the road overbridge. The bridge and building survive surprisingly little altered except that the waiting room is now open fronted, and there have usually been a loop and siding(s) of some sort. In early 15-in gauge days the yard was used as a general work area with a nissen hut engine shed. Currently it forms the second operational passing loop and the only one actually at a station; an island platform allows passenger interchange.

IRTON ROAD – BECKFOOT

It is always surprising, on a line that generally climbs into the hills, that the next section, sweeping round Long Yocking How, is actually mostly downgrade. The reason is that the railway here has deserted the River Mite and is crossing a dry valley to join the Esk which it will follow to its terminus. Irton Road is at one end of the village; at the other is. . .Eskdale Green station (or, rather, currently The Green since the prefix apparently confused passengers). Not many minor villages have two stations on the same line of railway but Eskdale Green was a full station in 3 ft gauge days, with a siding facing to Ravenglass, the usual low platform and a wooden booking-office-cum-shelter. Eventually this blew down and it was shelterless until the R & E R Preservation Society's West Yorkshire Group built (and maintained) a handsome waiting shelter and rustic platform.

Eskdale Green is just over a hump and there is a short downgrade as the line passes beneath the valley road by a stone-built bridge dating from 3 ft gauge days before once more starting to climb along the Esk valley. Hollinghow Bank, by milepost 5, includes a sharp but straight stretch of 1 in 36 (nominal) before the gradient eases beside remains of the ill-fated Fisherground Quarry of the late 1880s. Nature has covered most of the evidence though, till recently, fenced land indicated the probable junction as trailing to Ravenglass with a dead-end headshunt. The former—quite gentle—incline can be traced in a scrubby wood and what must have been the quarry face rises above a flat floor. There is then a short drop before the line crosses a farm track on the level, rounds Fisherground Corner (named from the farm below) and curves into the third—Fisherground—crossing loop. Unusually, right-hand running is employed here so that down trains approaching over a sharp curve have a straight run into the loop. The layout is, perhaps, not ideal since the original 3 ft gauge line's watering point, still used, is east of the loop exit and a recently installed halt to serve Fisherground camp site is yet further east. It is almost opposite the remains of an incline from the former Ban Garth mine which certainly predates even the 3 ft gauge, though it is noted as having been 'extended down to the railway' in 1874.

From Fisherground, the line, sticking closely to the former 3 ft gauge roadbed, twists and turns through the valley, curving under an access bridge for Spout House farm (5.7m) which lies below and to the right; one useful legacy of the old line is that the present one has little trouble with clearances. Until 1963, the track made a sharp reverse curve round Hollingshead bluff, which must have severely taxed the broader gauge equipment. It was very scenic but in that year a cutting—Gilbert's Cutting after its sponsor—was cut through the bluff on a steady left-hand curve. There is, if anything, a slight fall through the cutting and then a gentle climb past the former Beckfoot Quarry to the left. 3 ft gauge arrangements are not recorded, the existing smithy ruins dating from the 1920s and the compressor house from the late 1940s, but the 15 inch gauge had a facing junction leading to a fan of sidings in the quarry and a trailing siding for local transhipment to lorries in the road. Another climb beside the valley road brings us to Beckfoot Halt alongside the former Stanley Ghyll Hotel, now a CHA holiday centre. The 3 ft gauge had a station here, mainly to serve mines and Stanley properties and because it was the last contact with the valley road. It had the usual facing siding, on the north side, a platform and a shelter of the usual wooden pattern—but one which (shades of the metropolis!) boasted automatic vending machines. How many people, one wonders, had an urge to purchase chocolate at this out-of-the-way spot? It clearly had importance for on the south side, between rail and road, was a stone loading bank with a small, tarred goods shed on it and, in later years, some trains terminated here. The early 15 inch gauge had a terminus here also, with a run-round loop on the old formation and the place is still a conditional halt with a platform on the south side.

THE TOP END – BOOT & DALEGARTH

The final climb, at 1 in 38 through Beckfoot Wood, starts here, the line first crossing a service road which runs alongside to the far end. On the far left, buried in the wood, are relics of the bothies or 'tarpaulined huts' where formerly itinerant miners and quarrymen dossed down before more permanent accommodation was built. That, a row of what used to be typical workers' cottages, is at the wood's end where the 3 ft gauge line climbed on to Boot and Donaldson's Gill Force tramway had its junction. Let us deal with the Boot line first, which can be done in the past tense for it has been lifted since the early 1920s. It climbed east at a steady 1 in 36/1 in 38 behind the cottages and along the northern fell for about half a mile to end at a station above Boot village; its trackbed is still a pleasant walk. At Boot, joined to the village below only by a stony track, was a single platform on the south side with the standard wood shelter and with a one-hole privy hut thriftily perched astride a streamlet that passed beneath the track at the western end. The layout appears to have varied from time to time but always included a loop and a siding on the north side running under ore-tipping shutes from the mines loading bank. At this length of time the mines layout is conjectural but a track must have run east by the former mine company's office and smithy to join the Nab Gill incline. This also is not now clear, having been altered and overlaid from time to time and the gentle embankment sloping across its foot may not have been a rail track at all but a sled road.

In 1916 the 15 inch gauge initially stopped short at Beckfoot but there is evidence that by July 1917 the line had been pushed right through to Boot and there are photos of more than one layout. Certainly by the end of 1918, the extra climb had been found too taxing and the line was cut back to Dalegarth cottages where a terminus was made in front of them on the former Gill Force route. A run-round loop was put in, a tea room opened in the cottages, but the spot was not well sited for attracting casual traffic. Consequently, in 1926, the line was extended further over the old tramway, crossing Whillan Beck to a new terminus by the valley road. This site, though operationally more convenient, is very narrow, requiring the turntable to be sited at the dead-end and—in recent years—causing problems with long locomotives. Initially three tracks were installed but clearances proved very tight and for most of its life the station has had two roads, latterly with an island platform to allow two trains to load simultaneously. The current building, albeit modified, was a 'temporary' one bought in November 1927 and the original short platform was later extended, all these facilities being built out on piles. In 1979 the station was renamed Eskdale (Dalegarth).

The former Gill Force mines tramway of the 3 ft gauge period followed the same route up to this point, starting from a simple junction near Dalegarth cottages. It then crossed the road on the level and ran across fields to the Esk at Underbank. The initial stretch is not traceable since its enclosing walls have been removed though a built-up gap in the field wall shows where it entered. From the farm track leading to St Catherine's Church, however, the trackbed can be seen curving away between stone walls, through the corner of a wood and then on a man-made ledge above the river. Just before it crosses the Esk by a bridge whose girders are still extant, is a clearly visible loop site. The exact arrangement is unclear but debris and 1890s OS maps suggest there was a transhipment point here between 3 ft gauge and the 2 ft gauge known to have existed below ground. The position is discussed in chapter 2.

TICKETS

3 ft gauge. The R & E used standard Edmondson tickets with the common colours of white (1st single); yellow/white (1st return); purple (3rd single); and blue/red (3rd return). Special parliamentary tickets were issued for the first train of the day, coloured green in early years and purple later, and excursion tickets, quaintly titled 'pleasure party' tickets in blue and white were issued in conjunction with paper coupons. It seems probable that, because of the difficulties of reserving accommodation at peak periods, the leader had the coupon as a receipt and his party were then issued individual tickets to display to the guard. There were also some day returns which were normal issues printed with 'Available on day of issue only'. Dog tickets were blue.

Lettering and conditions of issue had their peculiarities. In particular, the date stamp was odd in incorporating an indication of the actual departure for which it was issued. Thus a stamp 05.AUG.18.2 indicated 1905, 18 August, second train of the day.

The Eskdale Railway Company never issued tickets as passengers were not officially carried during its operation of the line.

15 in gauge. Early tickets were generally of Edmondson pattern and through tickets from the Furness LMS were issued particularly for the latter's Wastwater Tour. No class indication was given except on the main-line portion of through tickets, but adult and child fares were sometimes quoted and internal tickets carried advertisements on the back.

After 1925, the new régime introduced Williamson thin card tickets of simplified pattern which were produced in rolls and torn off as required. The main point of interest was the regulation of passengers at peak periods, restricting their return from Dalegarth by specified trains, with overprinted tickets in easily-recognised colours. The general pattern has remained much the same ever since, although the titling was changed from Narrow Gauge Railways to Ravenglass & Eskdale Railway on tickets from 1946 onwards. Since 1960 the new operating company has continued to use the same pattern but has further simplified matters by grouping destinations and thus reducing the number of different tickets. It has also introduced a free privilege ticket for R & E R P S members and a quarter-fare ticket for use by railwaymen. Railway-type tickets have been re-introduced in the last few years for all but full round trips, tickets for which remain of the tear-off variety.

ATLAS OF THE LINE
(See following pages)

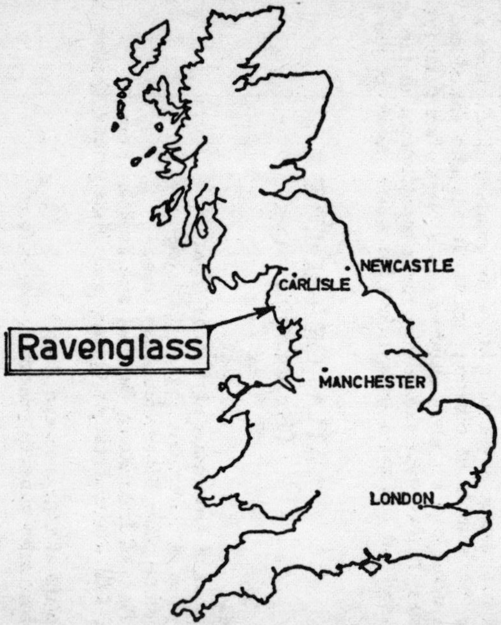

KEY TO PLANS

BO	Booking Office
CS	Carriage Shed
ES	Engine Shed
GS	Goods Shed
LC	Level Crossing
S	Shelter
SB	Station Building
WB	Weigh-bridge
WT.	Water Tank
	Platform
	Exact layout uncertain
1964	Date of installation

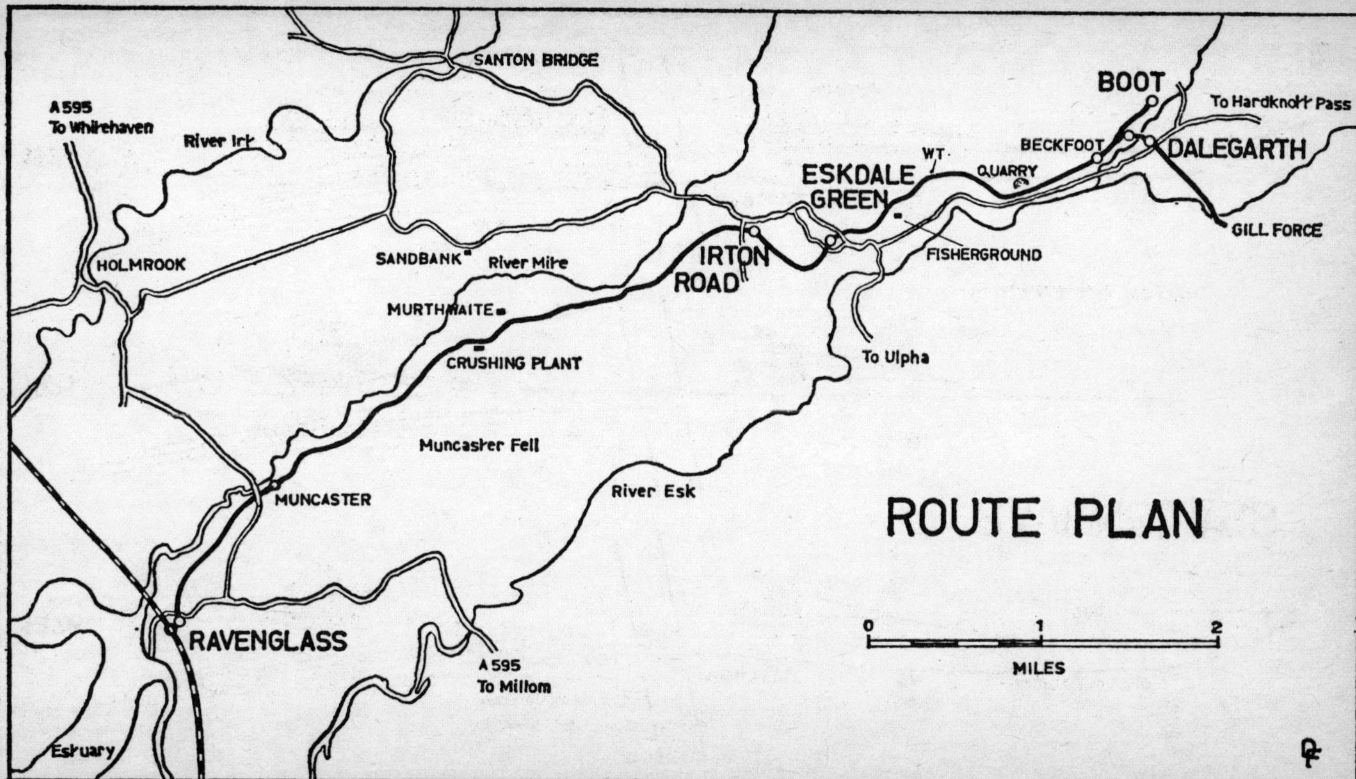
ROUTE PLAN
SANTON BRIDGE
A595
To Whitehaven
River Irt
HOLMROOK
SANDBANK
River Mite
MURTHWAITE
CRUSHING PLANT
Muncaster Fell
MUNCASTER
RAVENGLASS
Estuary
A595
To Millom
River Esk
IRTON
ROAD
ESKDALE
GREEN
WT.
FISHERGROUND
To Ulpha
QUARRY
BECKFOOT
BOOT
DALEGARTH
To Hardknott Pass
GILL FORCE
0
1
2
MILES

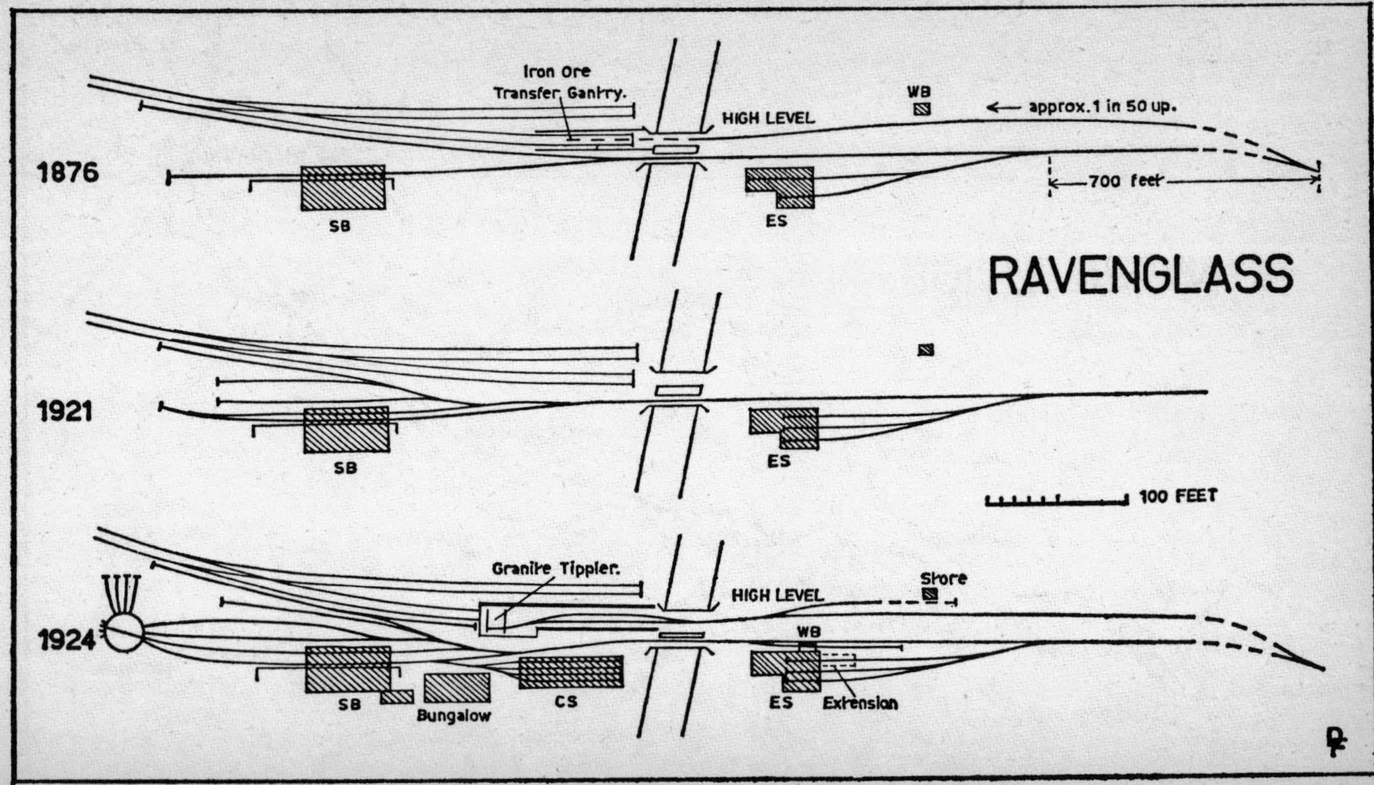
RAVENGLASS
1876
Iron Ore
Transfer Gantry.
HIGH LEVEL
WB
approx. 1 in 50 up.
700 feet
SB
ES
1921
SB
ES
100 FEET
1924
Granite Tippler.
HIGH LEVEL
Store
WB
SB
Bungalow
CS
ES
Extension

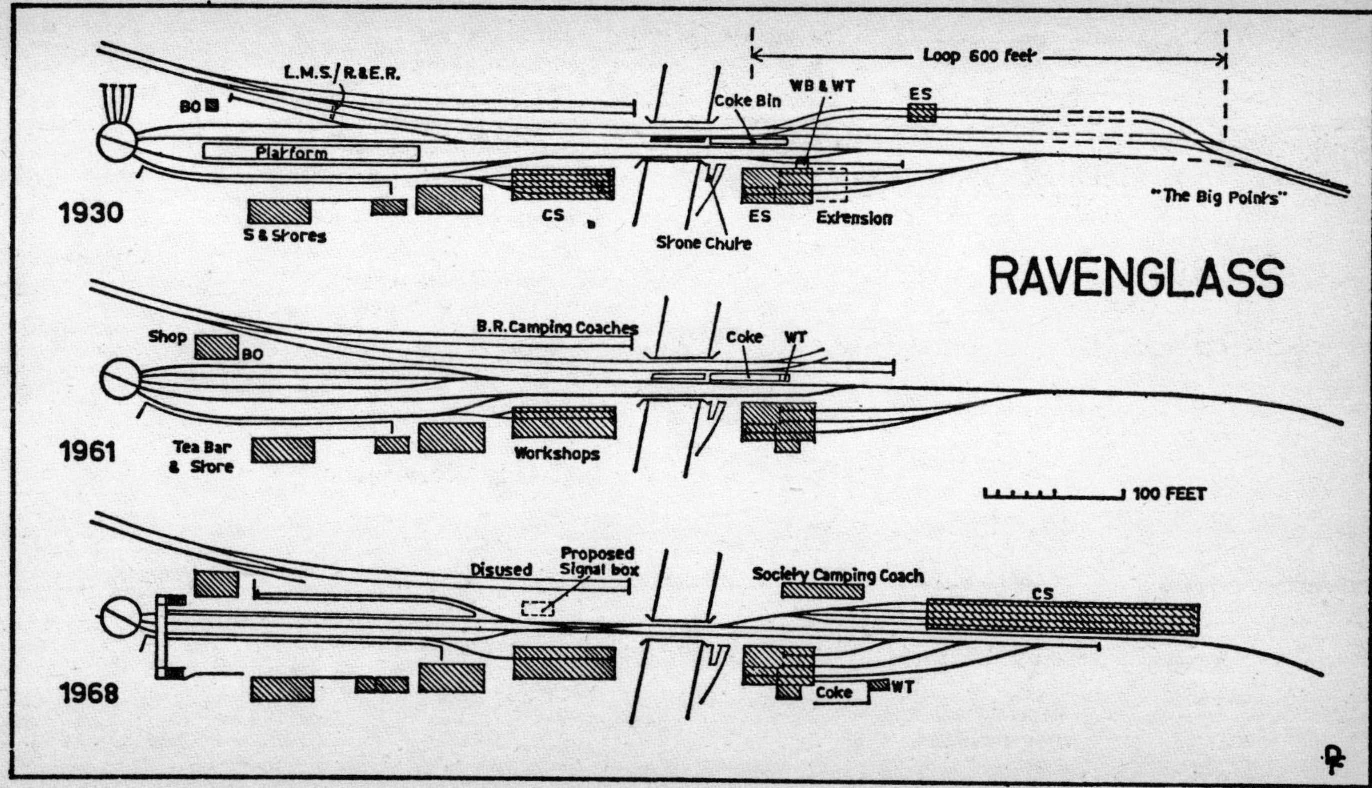
RAVENGLASS
1930
L.M.S./R.&E.R.
BO
Platform
S & Stores
CS
Coke Bin
WB & WT
ES
Loop 600 feet
Stone Chute
ES
Extension
"The Big Points"
1961
Shop
BO
B.R. Camping Coaches
Coke
WT
Tea Bar & Store
Workshops
100 FEET
1968
Disused
Proposed Signal box
Society Camping Coach
CS
Coke
WT

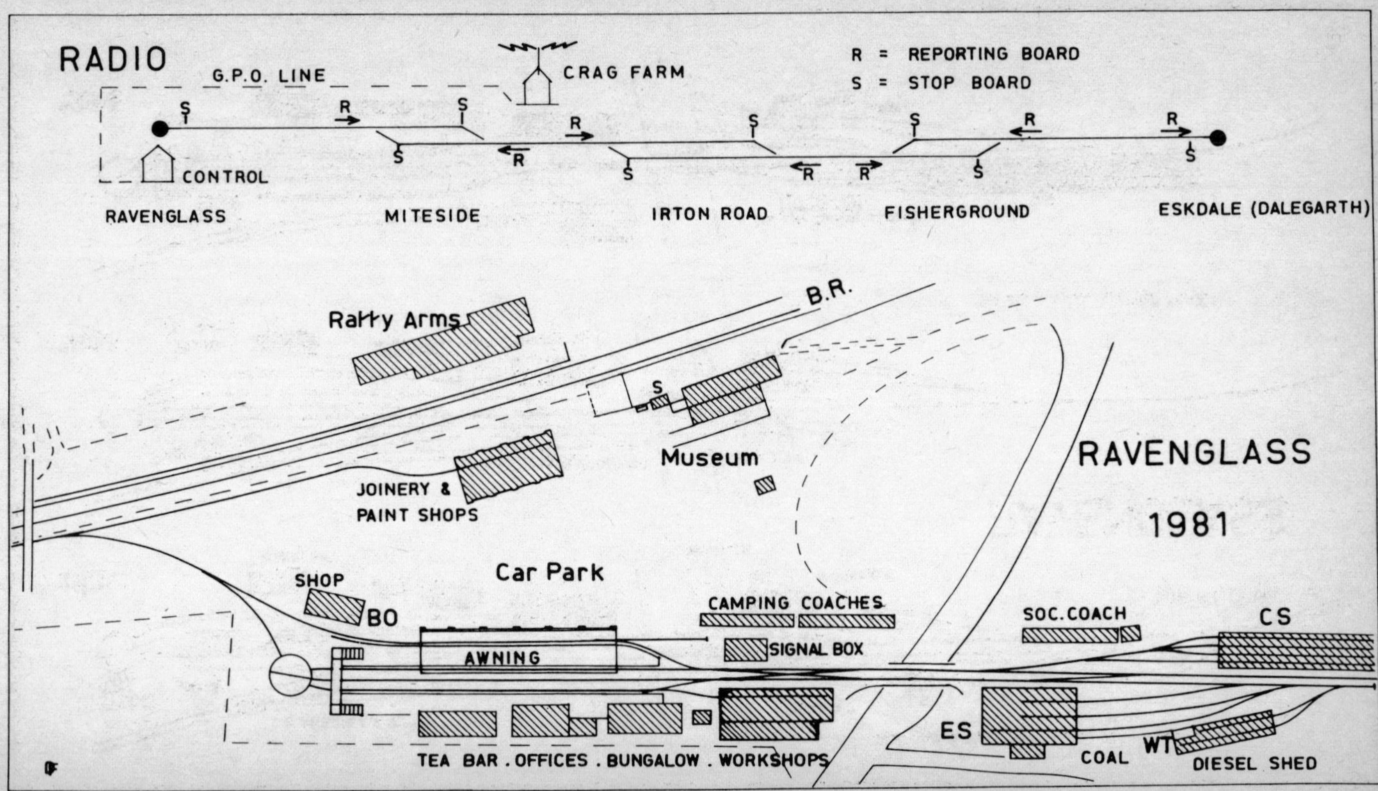
RADIO
G.P.O. LINE
CRAG FARM
R = REPORTING BOARD
S = STOP BOARD
CONTROL
RAVENGLASS
MITESIDE
IRTON ROAD
FISHERGROUND
ESKDALE (DALEGARTH)
B.R.
Ratty Arms
Museum
JOINERY & PAINT SHOPS
RAVENGLASS 1981
Car Park
SHOP
BO
CAMPING COACHES
SOC. COACH
CS
AWNING
SIGNAL BOX
ES
COAL
WT
DIESEL SHED
TEA BAR . OFFICES . BUNGALOW . WORKSHOPS

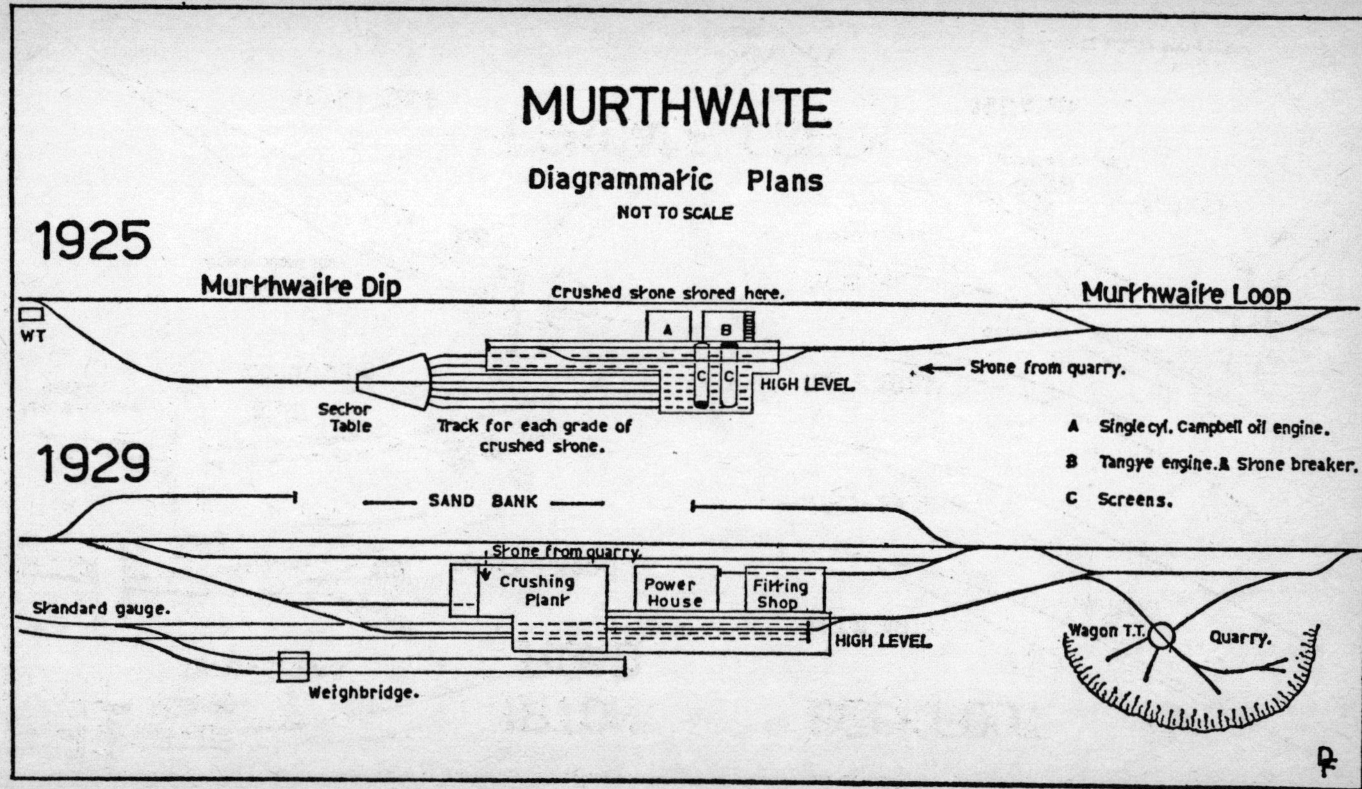
MURTHWAITE
Diagrammatic Plans
NOT TO SCALE
1925
Murthwaite Dip
Crushed stone stored here.
Murthwaite Loop
WT
A
B
C
C
Stone from quarry.
HIGH LEVEL
Sector Table
Track for each grade of crushed stone.
A Single cyl. Campbell oil engine.
B Tangye engine. & Stone breaker.
C Screens.
1929
SAND BANK
Stone from quarry.
Crushing Plant
Power House
Fitting Shop
Standard gauge.
HIGH LEVEL
Wagon T.T.
Quarry.
Weighbridge.

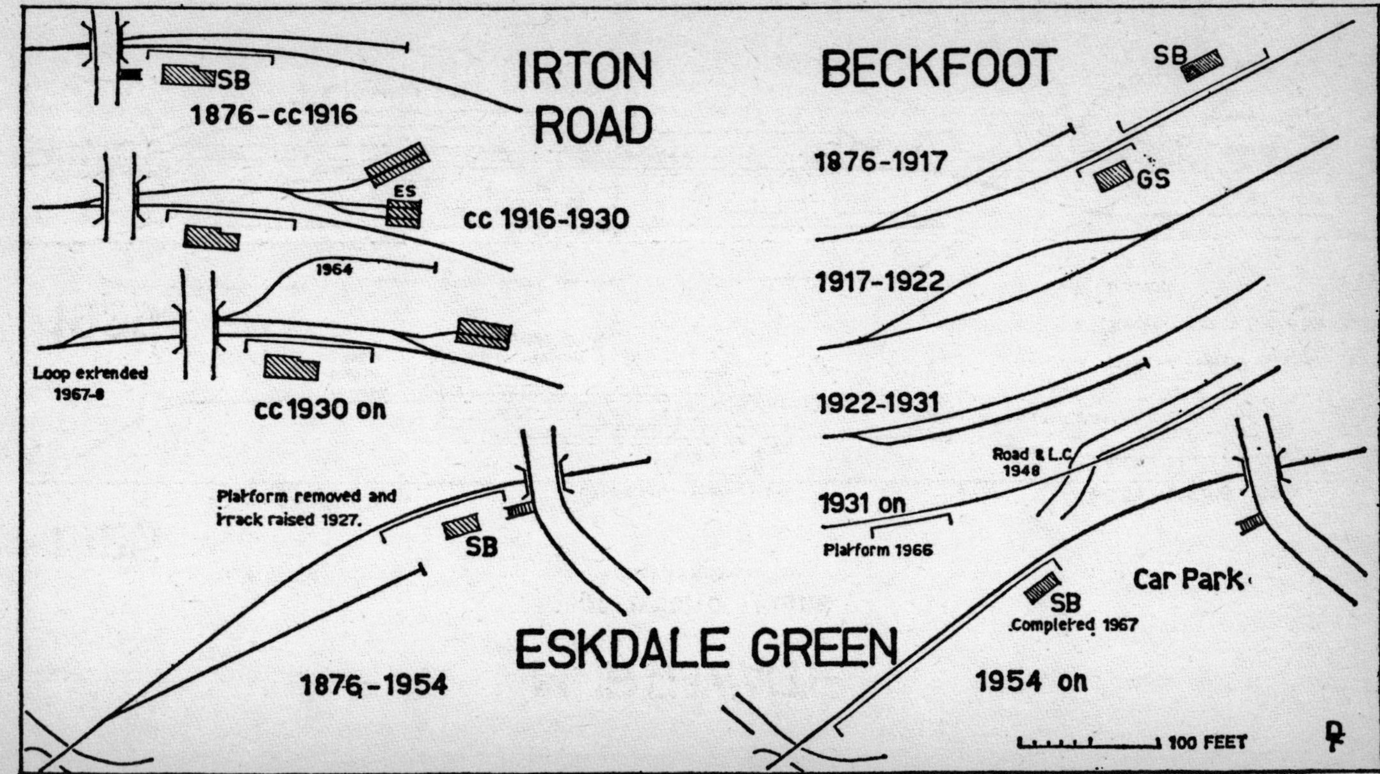

IRTON ROAD
SB
1876-cc1916
ES
cc 1916-1930
1964
Loop extended 1967-8
cc1930 on
BECKFOOT
SB
GS
1876-1917
1917-1922
1922-1931
Road & L.C. 1948
1931 on
Platform 1966
Platform removed and track raised 1927.
SB
ESKDALE GREEN
1876-1954
Car Park
SB
Completed 1967
1954 on
100 FEET

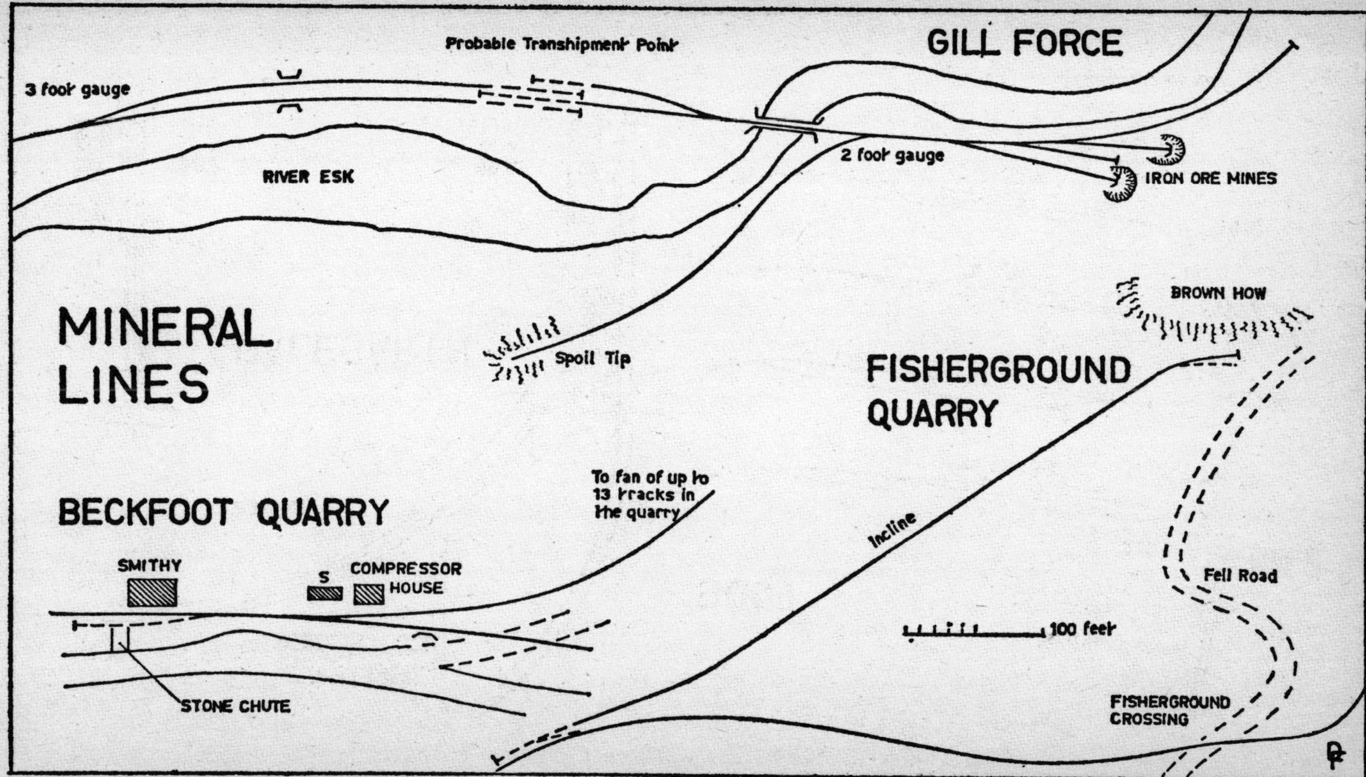

GILL FORCE
Probable Transhipment Point
3 foot gauge
2 foot gauge
IRON ORE MINES
RIVER ESK
MINERAL
LINES
Spoil Tip
BROWN HOW
FISHERGROUND
QUARRY
BECKFOOT QUARRY
To fan of up to
13 tracks in
the quarry
Incline
SMITHY
S
COMPRESSOR
HOUSE
STONE CHUTE
Fell Road
100 feet
FISHERGROUND
CROSSING

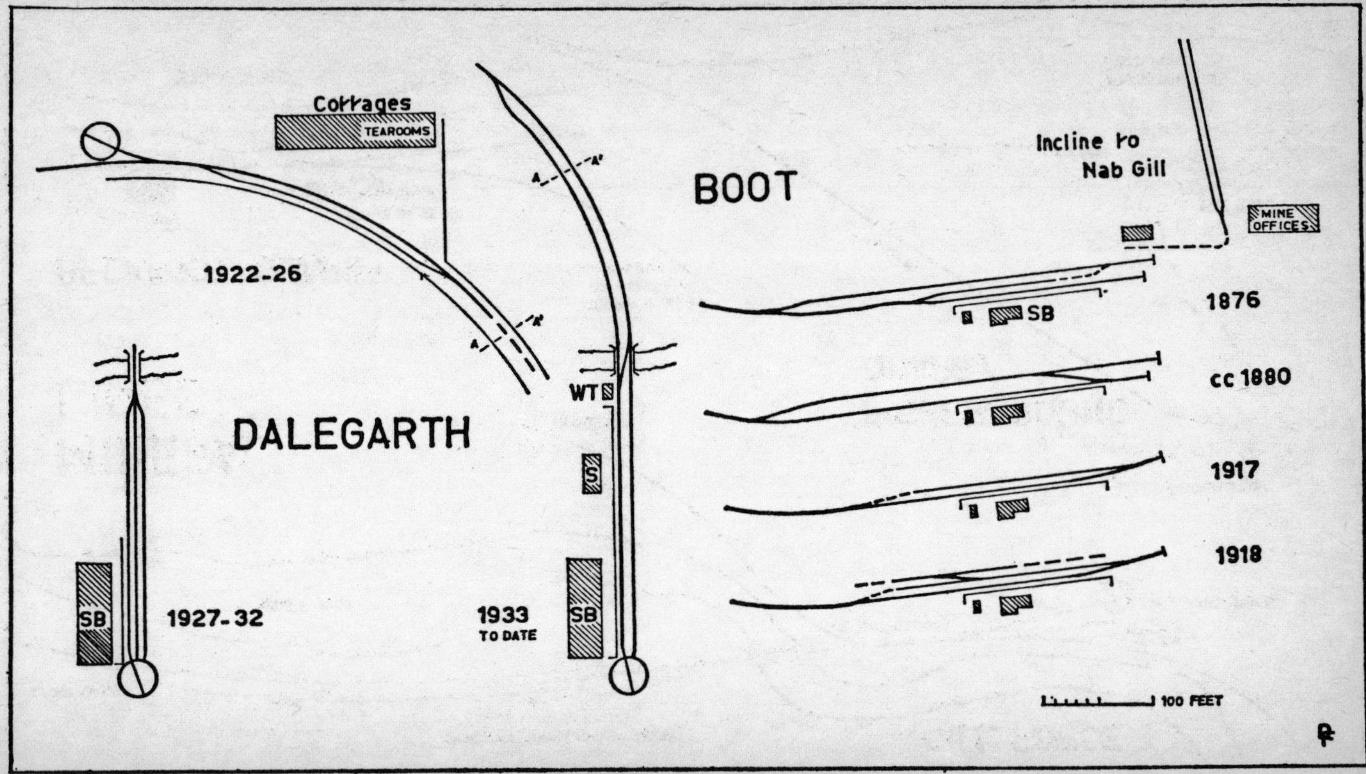

BOOT
Incline to
Nab Gill
MINE OFFICES
SB
1876
cc 1880
1917
1918
100 FEET
DALEGARTH
Cottages
TEAROOMS
1922-26
WT
S
SB
1933
TO DATE
SB
1927-32

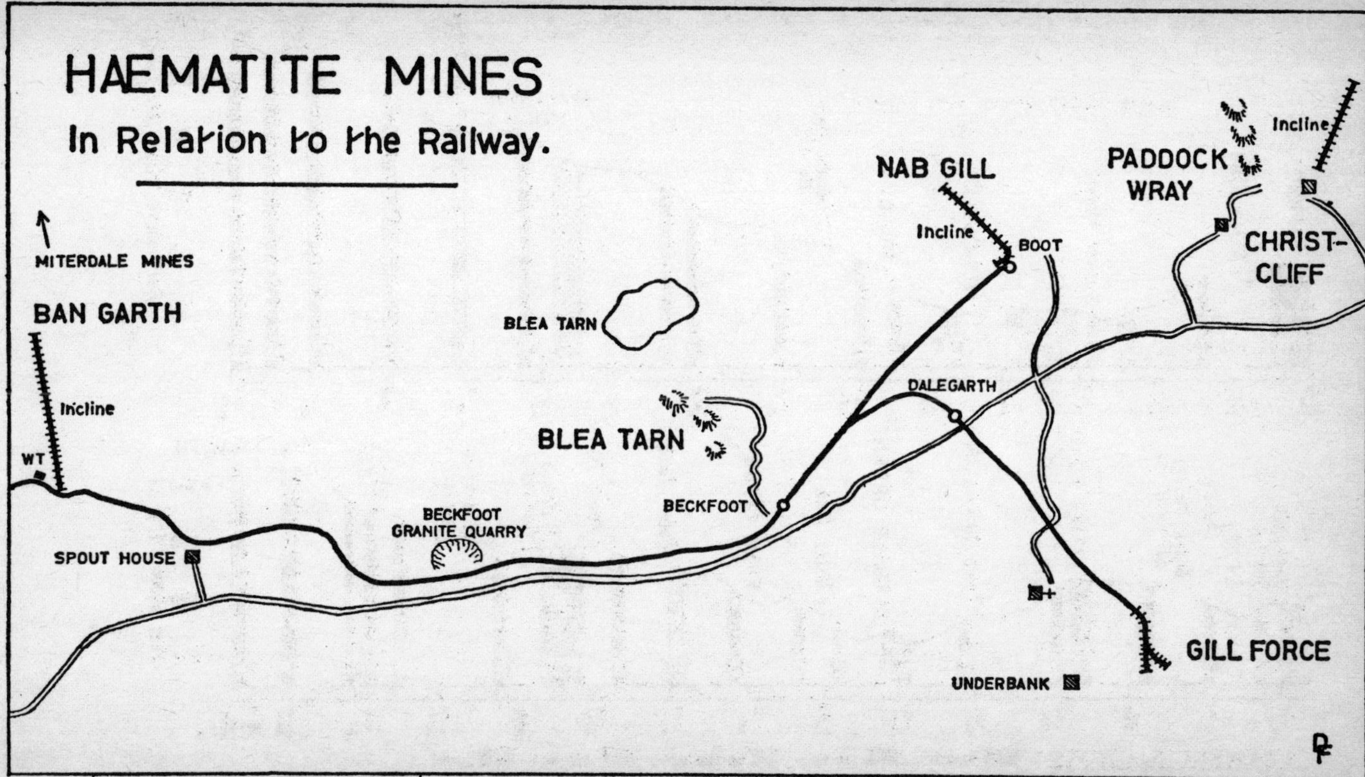
HAEMATITE MINES
In Relation to the Railway.
MITERDALE MINES
BAN GARTH
Incline
WT
SPOUT HOUSE
BECKFOOT
GRANITE QUARRY
BLEA TARN
BLEA TARN
BECKFOOT
DALEGARTH
NAB GILL
Incline
BOOT
PADDOCK
WRAY
Incline
CHRIST-
CLIFF
GILL FORCE
UNDERBANK
DF

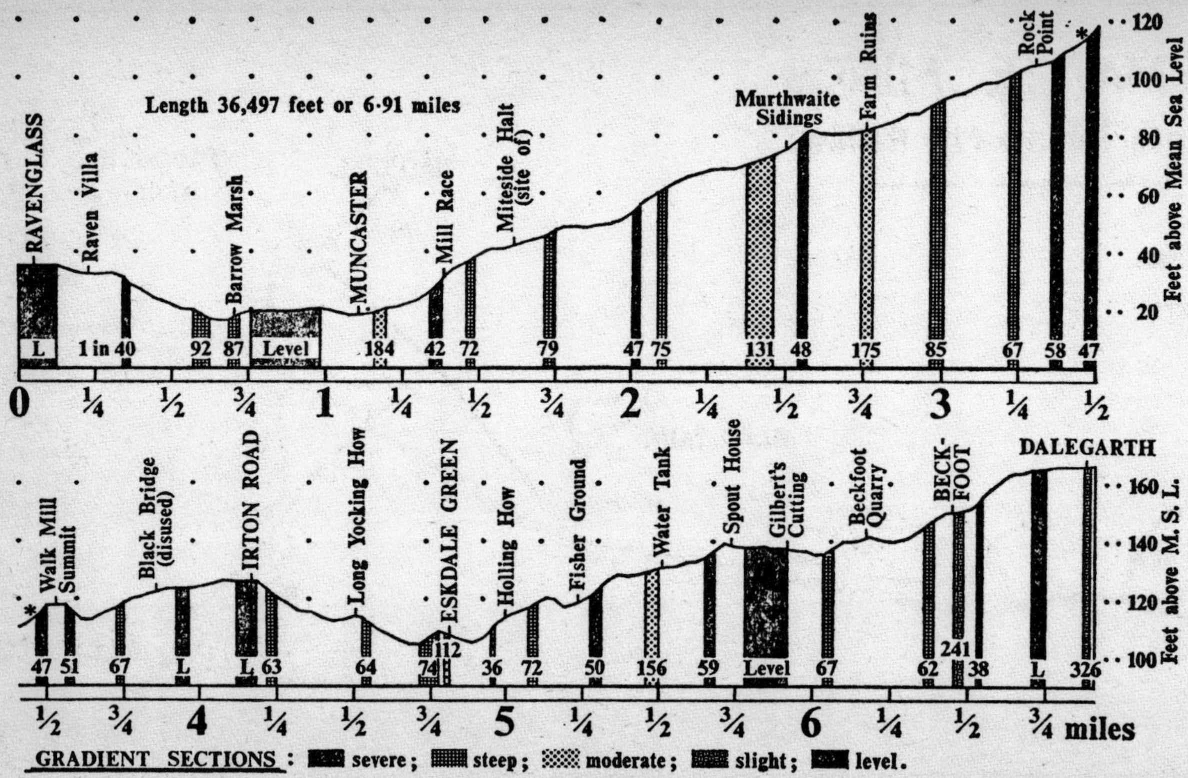
Length 36,497 feet or 6·91 miles
RAVENGLASS
Raven Villa
Barrow Marsh
MUNCASTER
Mill Race
Miteside Halt (site of)
Murthwaite Sidings
Farm Ruins
Rock Point
L
1 in 40
92
87
Level
184
42
72
79
47
75
131
48
175
85
67
58
47
0
¼
½
¾
1
2
3
20
40
60
80
100
120
Feet above Mean Sea Level
Walk Mill
Summit
Black Bridge (disused)
IRTON ROAD
Long Yocking How
ESKDALE GREEN
Holling How
Fisher Ground
Water Tank
Spout House
Gilbert's Cutting
Beckfoot Quarry
BECK-FOOT
DALEGARTH
47
51
67
L
63
64
74
112
36
72
50
156
59
Level
67
62
241
38
L
326
4
5
6
miles
100
120
140
160
Feet above M. S. L.
GRADIENT SECTIONS: severe; steep; moderate; slight; level.

Bibliography

There is comparatively little definitive published material on the R & E R and most of the material in this book has been gathered from collections of documents in public and private archives which it is impossible to catalogue here. The main sources of published material are given below but readers are warned that they are in some cases misleading.

Minimum Gauge Railways (Sir A. P. Heywood), published by author, 3rd edn., 1894
The Ravenglass & Eskdale Railway (H. Greenly), R & E R Company, 1923
'Ratty' (W. McGowan Gradon), published by author, 1947
ABC of Narrow Gauge Railways (W. J. K. Davies), Ian Allan Limited, 1961
Miniature Railways (R. Butterell) Ian Allan Limited, 1964
Miniature Steam Locomotives (G. Woodcock), David & Charles, 1964

The following periodicals were consulted: *R & E R Newsletter,* 1960—on; *Locomotive* (especially the series of articles by Whitehead, early 1942); *Railway Magazine; Railway News* for 2 and 16 September 1919; *Railway World; The Wide World.* Newspapers included *Cumberland Pacquet* and *Whitehaven News.*

The main collections of documents are:
Leconfield Estate Papers; Company Files for Narrow Gauge Railways Limited; Ravenglass & Eskdale Railway Company; Whitehaven Iron Mines Limited; South Cumberland Iron Co Limited; Chancery Papers; Board of Trade Returns; Acts of Parliament; Cumberland Archives at Carlisle.

Index